*The
Modern Jewish
Guide to
Dating and Mating*

HOW TO

WOO A

JEW

Tamar Caspi

SEAL PRESS

HOW TO WOO A JEW
The Modern Jewish Guide to Dating and Mating
Copyright © 2014 Tamar Caspi

Published by
Seal Press
A Member of the Perseus Books Group
1700 Fourth Street
Berkeley, California
www.sealpress.com

Library of Congress Cataloging-in-Publication Data

Caspi, Tamar.
How to woo a Jew : the modern Jewish guide to dating and mating / Tamar Caspi.
pages cm
ISBN 978-1-58005-500-0 (pbk.)
1. Man-woman relationships. 2. Dating (Social customs) I. Title.
HQ801.C3267 2014
306.73—dc23
2013034425

10 9 8 7 6 5 4 3 2 1

Cover design by Faceout Studio, Tim Green
Interior design by Tabitha Lahr
Page 174 illustration icons © adamson/123rf.com
Printed in the United States of America
Distributed by Publishers Group West

To my second chance . . .

✡ CONTENTS ▶

✦ INTRODUCTION ➤

WHEN I WAS IN MY midtwenties I was, in retrospect, looking for something I thought I wanted. I had this fantasy idea of how I would meet someone and how we would live happily ever after with our adorable kids and a big house full of nice things. I wanted romance and chemistry and some fun hobbies we both enjoyed. I wanted someone Jewish who envisioned raising kids with the same Jewish values and traditions I held and practiced. I wanted someone I was attracted to, of course, but I did understand that attraction would grow deeper over time. Yet I never truly thought about how that would all happen. I thought about both of us needing to be successful in order to obtain this cushy lifestyle, but I didn't think about finding a man who would be able to stand strong next to me during life's inevitable trivialities. I didn't think about looking at men with the mind-set of "is he a fair fighter?" or "does he react instinctively or intuitively?" or "what kind of co-parent will he be?" And at the end of the day, those are very important aspects to consider.

Back then, I was actively dating and doling out advice to friends left and right even though I was just as confused as they were, trying to figure out how to effectively and successfully date. I could help my friends, but I couldn't help myself. I received the opportunity to begin writing a monthly column about Jewish dating when I was twenty-seven, which quickly evolved into an internationally syndicated column. And while I was writing and the column was growing in popularity, I finally ended up meeting who I thought was my *beshert*, or my destiny. I was in another country and fell so hard and so fast for this man that before you could blink an eye I was on a plane and moving to Israel to be with him. Our story was a fairy tale, and I relished in believing that it was my expertise in dating that led me to be able to "just know" that he was my intended.

Just one month earlier, there I was, on vacation in Israel, sitting at a bar in Tel Aviv celebrating a friend of a friend's birthday, and I was scanning the crowd, people watching, when it seemed as though a spotlight was shining on a guy who I had just seen walk in. I kept my eye trained on him, and it was as if we were connected by an invisible string as he walked directly toward me and sat down right next to me. Granted, he was also there for the same person's birthday, but I wouldn't find that out until later. After sending some very obvious signals that I was interested we began talking, and suddenly it was four o'clock in the morning and the stools were stacked on the bar and the floors were being washed. We exchanged phone numbers and made plans to meet up a mere eight hours later for lunch. That lunch date ended up lasting twenty-four hours with unending conversation, chemistry, and a clear connection. Lunch had led to a swim in the ocean, which led to a walk along the river, which led to dinner then dancing then breakfast before saying goodbye with the promise to see each other again before I left the country.

He called that afternoon, and after making plans to meet we agreed that I should try and extend my vacation by a few days so we could travel and spend more time together. After five days straight of being together, the last night of my trip arrived, and I was sadly packing to return to my life Stateside. That was when he turned to me and said, "I want to ask you a question but I'm afraid to ask it," and I responded, "If you're going to ask what I think you're going to ask, then ask it because I'm going to say yes but I need to hear you ask it," and so he asked, "Will you move here?" and I instantly said, "Yes!" We were elated, we were falling in love, and we didn't doubt for one second that we could have found our beshert at a bar one week ago. I moved to Israel just three weeks later, and we began our lives together.

I had seen enough of my contemporaries in the midst of marriages to know that life is not perfect. People fight. I've always said that those who don't fight have more problems than those that do because they most likely aren't being honest and are not communicating. So when my boyfriend and I began fighting, I thought, *We are a passionate couple who loves hard and fights hard, and as long as we are happier more of the time than we aren't then we are winning in this game of love.* I even did the math: Our fights would last a few days and would occur, at the time, once a month. So three days of fighting every thirty days meant that 90 percent of the time, we were happy. When the frequency of fights increased to twice a month, the percentage dropped to 80 percent, but that still meant we were happy the majority of the time. And I made myself believe that was enough.

The thing was, it was the type of fighting and the subject of the fighting and the source of the fighting and the lack of productiveness and respect within the fighting that was making it feel like during that 20 percent of the month, we had a virus seeping into our lives. We persevered through the fighting and relied on both the initial connection that brought us together and the life we were building together. Ten months after we met, we got engaged and planned a move back to the States, starting with a wedding in my hometown. The fighting was still there, though. It lingered and darkened what should have been one of the happiest and most exciting times in our lives. My train of thought was, *Not if, but when, we get through this, we will be a stronger couple and everything will settle down soon.* We moved to California three months later, got married two months after that, and I was sure that all the fighting would miraculously disappear.

But that doesn't happen. There is no magic potion. Marriage takes a lot of work to, well, make it work. And I now know I don't want a marriage that just "works." I want to have mutual love and respect and to have fun and most important to have a strong foundation with my partner so when tough circumstances arise we can get through them together. With marriage, the only hard work should be the effort going toward ensuring you make time for romance and a healthy sex life when life gets in the way; it should not be the actual getting along part. The thing is, you know if you get along or not long before you get married.

As logical as this seems, there are many barriers that can keep us from recognizing a relationship that is just not working. I can say that for me, along with my high hopes, there was also some ego that got in the way of leaving what I now know was an unhealthy relationship. After three years of marriage and giving birth to one amazing child, I am now divorced. But I don't have regrets. In fact, I feel even more qualified to write a book on dating because I've made my share of mistakes, I learned from them, and I grew as a person, a mother, a woman, and a dating expert. It's not just my divorce that lends me a greater breadth of knowledge but also the dating life I've led along the way, both pre- and postdivorce.

For the first ten years of my dating life before I met my ex-husband, I exclusively dated non-Jews. In fact, I was anti-Jew. I wanted nothing to do with the Brit Milah'ed, Bar Mitzvah'ed bunch. Marrying Jewish was what was expected of me, but, during Jewish summer camp, I had had bad social experiences with not only Jewish guys but girls, too, that turned me off to Jewish dating. True, we were all immature, hormonal teenagers, but when you're in the moment you think it's your whole world, and, in that world, I didn't like my options. My parents raised me to see everyone as equal, and, although I went to a Jewish elementary school, my extracurricular activities were held in our neighborhood, where I was exposed to different races and religions. To me, these friends were my friends by choice—not because they were also Jewish—and I liked that. By junior high and high school, all of my closest girlfriends weren't Jewish, and, for the most part, the guys we were meeting also weren't Jewish. Sure, I had Jewish guys asking me out, but they didn't excite me. I wanted to find my own path, not because it wasn't what was expected of me, but because I had found commonalities with these platonic and romantic friends based on what I believed at the time were deeper connections. I also knew that I was young and wanted to have fun and not take life so seriously—as in, not worry about how I was going to celebrate Rosh Hashanah ten years later.

I was raised in a traditional Jewish family with an Israeli father and an American-Jewish mother. They met when my mom made aliyah to Israel, but they returned to the States to start and raise their family in California. My sister, my brother, and I were blessed by a Rabbi when we were born, we attended Jewish Community

Center preschool, and we went to Jewish day school. We were Bar/Bat Mitzvah'ed and confirmed, and we went to Jewish summer camp. We celebrated Shabbat and every Jewish holiday and went to synagogue when it counted. We went to Israel regularly. My parents, grandparents, and extended family were all active in the Jewish community, giving of their time and money. In essence, we were raised with Judaism, Zionism, and Jewish pride running through our veins. I had all of that, but yet when I came of age I wasn't interested in dating Jewish men.

I felt that I was "Jewish enough" to pass on my religion—traditions, culture, language, faith, and so on—to my children even with a supposed future husband who wasn't Jewish. In high school I wasn't worried about how the boys I was dating felt about this, but in college I would ask boyfriends if they would convert or at least be supportive of me raising our kids Jewish. I wanted a Jewish family, but I was adamant about also being attracted to my husband, and, at that point in my life, well, I wasn't attracted to Jewish men, as weird as that sounds. Plenty of people have made interfaith marriages and families work, and I thought I could be one of those people.

When I was twenty-one and still holding fast to my decision to only date non-Jews, my best Jewish friend got married to a great Jewish guy. I was the maid of honor and was forbidden to bring a date unless he was Jewish. I went solo and was the only one wearing lavender taffeta at the single's table. Fast forward a few years later, and this best friend was having a baby. I was now an honorary auntie. And I was seeing firsthand what building a family, a home, and a marriage was really all about. I was almost twenty-five years old, had been disappointed by men more than I cared to think about, and was nearing a quarter-life crisis. Something needed to change, and I needed to be in control of that change. I realized that the life my friend and her husband had built wasn't a fairy tale; it was work. I knew marriages needed a strong foundation to be able to succeed, and, for my friend and her husband, their foundation was their faith. And then something clicked. I realized that for me, my foundation would also be my faith. I was a Jew, and I wanted to marry a Jew and start a Jewish family in a Jewish home and be active in the Jewish community.

Once I realized how important it was to me to marry someone Jewish—to start and raise a family with someone Jewish—I was hooked. I didn't want to do it just for the future of the Jewish people, and I didn't want to do it just because I thought it would be "easier," but also because—and most important because—it was what felt right for me.

I had heard my share of critique throughout the ten years leading up to this point, but at the time those comments did not engender the intended Jewish guilt—they only pushed me further away. I didn't want to hear about "finishing Hitler's work," or my "bubbe rolling over in her grave." Maybe it was all true, but it didn't make me want to return to the fray. But what I learned at twenty-four years old is that being a proud Jew who only dates within the faith is nothing to be ashamed of. Neither is dating non-Jews! But it's a difficult message to convey, because it's not as though I don't believe non-Jews are good enough—they were just no longer right for me. Innerfaith dating is important. And couples do make it work. Jews are a minority, and studies show that interfaith dating is becoming more and more popular. Yet we should still remember that it wasn't too many generations ago our people were nearly eliminated, and to this day we are in a constant battle to defend our existence, which means it's even more important to instill Jewish pride into future generations of Jews. Some people have been able to marry outside the faith and raise Jewish children, and that's truly great! Some Jewish couples have not instilled Judaism in their kids but have raised Israel-loving families. But sometimes that doesn't happen, and I had finally realized all of that and more. So with my newfound clarity, I moved from Los Angeles back to my hometown of San Diego, focused on furthering my career as a writer, and decided to date only Jewish men.

I signed up for JDate, the popular Jewish dating website, I started attending Jewish singles mixers, and I spread the word that I was interested in being set up. I looked back on my past relationships and I couldn't even imagine what I had seen in those men; my priorities had shifted and, as a result, the type of guy I was attracted to did as well. Non-Jews were now a no-no. I was available and I was open to meeting new men and willing to give any Jew a chance.

Well, just about any Jew. I wasn't that desperate. There were still physical traits I was attracted to and other preferences that I held in high esteem. I wanted a tall, handsome Jew. The handsome part would be easy enough; the tall part? Not so much. But for me it was one of my few nonnegotiables.

I discovered on dates with Jewish men that we often had a connection based on commonalities, traditions, and values that I hadn't found in previous relationships. It's that type of connection that creates a foundation upon which a couple can build a strong marriage.

Divorce rates are lower among innerfaith marriages, and that's a fact. I know that's a strong statement and that it's dripping with Jewish guilt, but, as I continued dating Jews, I started to see things that way. My perspective changed so drastically that year, and I know that's not the norm—most Jews either don't care what religion their intended is or they are already dating only Jews and just want to find their beshert already. Though my path was unconventional, I was able to learn so much from it. I ended up using JDate not just to meet men but also to learn more about myself and what I was looking for in a husband. It helped me find out who I wanted to be in a relationship with and how I wanted to be treated.

NOW, POSTDIVORCE, I've grown again, and as a dating single mother I can see that, yes, sharing a religion is important, but so are other elements that I wasn't aware of preparenthood. I now tell people without kids to date as if they are single parents and are looking for a step-parent for their children. It may sound extreme, but looking for someone who is "good with kids" just doesn't cut it. You need to agree on things such as: Do we want one of us to be a stay-at-home parent until the children are in elementary school? And if so, how do we look at finances when there's only one person bringing in an income? Do we want to send our kids to private Jewish school, and how are we going to afford to do so? What kind of discipline do we believe in? What is our parenting philosophy? Are both of us waking up in the night to feed the baby? Are we going to become a baby-wearing, co-sleeping household? Are we going to put the baby on a sleep schedule? Yes, these are things that nonparents, especially those in their twenties, often have not yet thought about, and that's the point. These are things you're going to have to deal with if you decide to have children, and if you and your intended don't have the same thought process or are not amenable to compromise, then you are probably going to be in for a long and unhappy life . . . or divorce. And it's not just the parenting realm, but other aspects of life as well, such as figuring out where you want to live (urban or rural?) and how you want to vacation (beach or touring?) and how you want to budget (joint everything or separate accounts?) and how you want to incorporate your Judaism (Shabbat every Friday or High Holy Days only?) and so forth. These are not first-date questions; they are nuggets of information you find out with time, though ideally prior to becoming too serious a couple. Of course, some people change when they actually become parents, and one never knows how they will react and adjust to this life-changing event, which is why it's even more important to go into marriage and parenthood as prepared as possible.

I realize there are situations when opposites attracting is a good thing, as we get to see different views on life and experience things we wouldn't have otherwise, but there are foundational personality characteristics and values in which being opposites will make life tough. For instance, a go-getter and a procrastinator, or an anxious person and a laid-back type, or a hunter and a vegan, and so on. This is not an "I want everything my ex-husband wasn't" issue because he did have many great traits, which is why I married him to begin with; rather, this is what I learned about how to proactively and effectively date.

When I started thinking about the type of man I would eventually want to look for once I was ready to date again after my divorce, I realized how deeply my priorities had shifted once more. Yes, I still wanted romance. Yes, I still wanted attraction (and height!). Yes, I still wanted an ambitious, successful man. But now, some traits that had been, alas, buried in my list had now catapulted to the top, including kindness and respect. You must ask yourself this about your intended: When you do fight, because you will fight, are you still being treated with kindness and respect? Something else I now put a higher ranking on is this: Who were the role models in this potential partner's life? I always said I wanted a man who was close to his mother, but I know now that's not enough. Instead, I want to know: What kind of role models were his parents in regard to being spouses and parenting? Some men say that they don't want to be the type of husband their own father was, yet their actions betray that statement.

Once I began considering these things, I had to ask myself these same types of questions. What kind of wife did I want to be the next time I (hopefully) got married? What traits in my own parents did I want to carry on, and which did I want to work on to make sure I broke the cycle of passing along something negative to the next generation? I knew I could not expect something from others that I was not willing to do myself.

So when my girlfriend called a few months after my divorce to offer to set me up, I declined. I wasn't ready. I was enjoying the lack of fighting and had also had so many life-changing revelations that I wanted to build upon that I didn't think I was quite healed enough yet to begin dating. The guy she knew—a divorced dad described as "a successful gentleman"—sounded great, and I knew if it was meant to be then he would still be available when I was ready. But a week later, that friend orchestrated what looked like a random run-in for the two of us, and there was an instant connection and attraction between us. I was attending a meeting on behalf of a Hebrew language charter school I was opening, and he was attending the same meeting as an interested parent even though he had already committed to sending his son to a different school for kindergarten.

He walked in to the meeting, and the moment I saw him, I felt butterflies—which I hadn't felt in what seemed like eons. After the meeting we began talking about our kids, and later he walked me to the car in the rain and asked if he could take me to dinner the next week. We exchanged numbers, and when I got into my car, the song "I Can't Help Falling in Love" was playing on the radio.

I had learned enough from my last random and instant connection and attraction nearly five years prior that I put up an additional guard to the one I already had up as a single parent. But there were definitely some impressive moves he employed that week that chipped away at my metaphoric wall: He called within a few days of meeting me to ask me out, he called again to confirm the date, he sent me flowers prior to our first date, he made all the plans for that date, and he picked me up at the exact time he said he would. He was wooing a Jew (me)!

Still, I had good reason to be cautious. I made sure that we didn't discuss our divorce stories for a few weeks, as it was important we got to know each other first before sharing our "baggage." We spoke about the kind of families we each came from, our Jewish backgrounds, and how we came to our respective careers. We spoke about our dating days and how what we were looking for in our midtwenties was—and was not—different nowadays. We played Jewish geography and marveled at the fact that we were both on JDate way back then and should have met but didn't. Throughout the getting-to-know-you stage, I didn't reveal too much about myself while still allowing him to get to know me. I've always prided myself on being an open book, but one of the lessons I've learned is that, at the beginning of a relationship, less is more. I didn't need to expose everything, positive or negative. I didn't need to know everything about him either. This needed to be a marathon, not a sprint. As long as he continued to treat me with kindness and respect, then we were on the right path.

After just a couple of weeks dating we planned a casual playdate to introduce our children to each other, where I got to see what kind of father he was, and he was able to determine the type of mother I am. These observations—and subsequent approvals—allowed us to take the relationship to the next stage. When we exchanged divorce stories, we each got to know another side of each other. We each had to internally ask ourselves if the reason the other got divorced was going to make an impact on our relationship and our future. How did he refer to his ex-wife? It was important to me that he still respected her as the mother of his son and that he still, after all the divorce drama, respected what they had as a couple while it was good. It was also important to me that he had learned both from the mistakes he made and from the marriage as a whole. I was incredibly skeptical while he told me his story, and I asked very productive and deliberate questions. I was encouraged by his answers as well as his attitude, honesty, and ownership of his role in the dissolution of the marriage.

The longer we've been together, the more I'm able to see how he handles serious and stressful issues, and I'm comforted by his re-actions. Is he perfect? No. And neither am I. The fact that we both know that and can admit that seems simple, but you'd be surprised at the number of people in the dating pool who think they're better than the rest.

Most of my adult life has been spent dating. My journey to finding a partner was not a smooth one nor was it a short one. It took years. It took frustration. It took heartache. It took a lot of growing. And then I found a love that would only come with that time and emotional growth. That journey is what this book is all about.

AS WITH MY DATING LIFE, my journey to becoming a writer has also been filled with many twists and turns. Writing was always my strong suit in school, but I never thought it could be my career. I was athletic, and I wanted to be a sports broadcaster. In paying my dues to become a reporter, I had to write, and it turned out I was indeed talented. Writing came naturally to me, and, though I was appreciated for my ability at various TV stations, writing about the news wasn't what I wanted to do for a living. So when San Diego's local Jewish paper was looking for a new singles columnist, I was given the opportunity to try my hand at opinion writing. And after writing my first column, I suddenly felt like I had found my niche. That gig led to a syndicated column in publications such as *The Jerusalem Post*, which led to an opportunity I never saw coming. I received an email from JDate thanking me for my articles. Then I received a follow-up email from JDate asking to speak with me. Then I got a phone call from JDate asking me to work for them. I accepted, and I became an "Official JDate Expert," answering JDaters' questions, doling out advice, and giving Extreme Profile Makeovers.

Today, I find myself with hundreds of articles I've written about dating advice, and I know there are future generations who could use the help. So compiling my articles into a guide to helping you find your beshert—or at least to give you a chuckle—is the obvious next step. This book is not just for young singles but also older singles, single parents, divorcés and divorcées, widows, and the happily wed, too. And if you're married, I hope you not only get a laugh from some of the stories but also see why you should give your single-and-dating friends some slack. It's not easy out there. They need compassion and support. They also need to realize they are not alone; there is a light at the end of the tunnel and they will reach it eventually.

I have had so many people from different walks of life email me asking for advice throughout my JDate career. To address the majority of the questions I've been asked over time in the span of this short guide, I have chosen to reference six different people's stories, and I will discuss how each person should handle the same situations nearly every single person encounters. In this book you'll meet Julie, a twenty-eight-year-old woman who thinks her biological clock is going to explode when she hits the big 3-0; Natalie, a woman in her early thirties who has never had to try to attract men yet doesn't know how to keep the good ones; Mike, a man who says he's finally ready to settle down in his midthirties yet continuously goes after the wrong type of woman; Lauren, a divorced single mom in her forties who hasn't dated in fifteen years; Beth, a woman approaching fifty who has never been married and has had to accept she won't have children while exploring her sexuality; and David, a prematurely widowed dad in his early sixties who is youthful-looking and active though having problems finding a contemporary who can match up with him. In these six characters there are a range of backgrounds and personalities to which everyone can relate, and therefore all readers should be able to apply my advice to their own circumstances.

Chapter 1

✱ SINGLE BUT NOT QUITE READY ➤
TO MINGLE

SO YOU'RE SINGLE AND YOU think you're ready to mingle. Dating is not easy, and at times it's not fun. Chances are you will not meet your beshert on the first date. In fact, chances are it will take dozens and dozens of dates before you meet the person you end up marrying. And it takes a lot more than just being excited at the prospect of meeting someone to be prepared for what will no doubt be a rocky road. You will get rejected, you will get depressed, you will get frustrated, and you will get your heart broken. You will also have times where you are made to feel like the most wonderful and beautiful person to walk the face of this earth, and yet you will want nothing to do with the person who makes you feel that way. And then you'll doubt yourself for not having chemistry with someone who makes you feel so amazing all the time. And then you'll try and pretend to feel something for this person because you think that is what's best for you.

Does this all sound too dramatic or too unrealistic for you and your life? Think you're better than this merry-go-round? You'd be surprised what happens once you're knee-deep in the dating world. It can suck. It's not all roses and chocolate-covered strawberries. Sometimes though, it can be exhilarating, because when you meet that "one" (or more—there's more than likely more than just one "one") who makes your stomach flutter and your heart skip a beat and your brain turn to mush and your mouth water, it will all be worth it. But how will you know when the someone who causes you to have a visceral reaction is the right one and not just someone who knows what to say and when to say it?

Follow a few steps for preparing to put yourself out there, whether you're a naive single in your twenties, or you're in your thirties and deafened by the sound of your biological clock ticking, or you're a divorced parent in your forties looking for not only a spouse but also a step-parent, or you're an all-too-young widow looking for a companion to enjoy retirement with. Regardless of your situation, you need to first remind yourself why you want to be one half of a couple and make sure it's for the right reasons. Your reasons for dating will be written in plain sight across your forehead whether you like it or not. If you're constantly wondering why perfectly eligible singles aren't jiving with you, then maybe your purpose in dating isn't genuine and you're putting off the wrong vibe. Do you want to share your life with someone, grow old with the same someone, and start a family with the same someone? Or are you just sick of being the fifth wheel, sick of sitting at the single's tables, and sick of going home to an empty house? Figure it out because you're going to get whatever it is you put out there.

When you're not sure about the kind of person you're looking for and you're not sure why you're even out there looking, your doubt and cynicism will be apparent. We can usually tell when someone is not done playing the field, when he or she is still looking to have fun and is not yet ready to find a partner and settle down. On the flip side, we can also tell when someone is either deafened by her—or his!—biological clock and is desperate to just get married already. As for the kind of people who will pursue you after you've made it clear that you aren't into them? Well, we all know people often like what they can't have. Don't fall into these situations if you don't want to attract these types of people. Make sure you know what your endgame goal is—a fun time, a serious relationship, and so on—and emote that on your face and in your body language.

Here are a few hypothetical situations in which to imagine yourself in order to figure out how ready you are for a relationship. There is no right or wrong answer; this is how you feel right now, and in a few months you may answer the questions differently:

- You meet someone, and you mutually experience attraction as well as intense feelings. How quickly would you be able to stop seeing other people and commit to a monogamous relationship?

- After getting dumped, do you spend the next month moping around or do you put your big-kid undies on and get back out there?

- Do you look at loving couples with envy or pity in your eyes?

- Are you willing to dedicate both your Friday and Saturday nights to quality dates rather than partying with your friends?

- Do you think $35 a month for an online dating subscription is a great investment or a waste of money?

- Would you be willing to change anything about yourself for the sake of a relationship?

- Are you scared of marriage or excited by the prospect of meeting your forever partner?

- Do you need a partner, or do you want a partner?

- Whose relationship would you emulate? Your parents'? Your friend's parents'? Your sibling's in-laws'?

- How do you feel about children? Would you marry someone with children? What parenting philosophy do you believe in?

Once you have figured out what kind of relationship you're looking for, what you're willing to do for said relationship, and who you want to be in a relationship with, you then need to figure out what kind of person you are looking for. To do that, you first need to realistically quantify what exactly you are bringing to the table in a relationship. This is difficult, I know. Don't focus on the looks department because pretty or ugly, skinny or fat, tall or short, and so on are not what relationships are built upon. Your thought process needs to also include kindness, humor, education and career aspirations, manners, family, friends, hobbies, and especially overall attitude and self-confidence. So how does someone subjectively quantify themselves?

According to *The Beauty Prescription*, cowritten by Debra Luftman, MD, a Beverly Hills dermatologist, and Eva Ritvo, MD, a South Beach psychiatrist, others see you as 20 percent more attractive than you see yourself because, when you look in the mirror, all you see is your reflection, while others see your personality and inner beauty when they look at you. So now that you know others perceive you as more attractive than you perceive yourself, you should be able to have more confidence. Self-esteem plays a huge role in dating, and by having some introspection, you will also be able to figure out what you may need to work on to be a higher-quality dating prospect. Whether it's gaining the confidence to go after a promotion at work, or working out more often instead of constantly moaning about how out of shape you are, or getting a makeover (either physical or mental . . . or both), these are things you've probably needed to do for yourself for a long time. Do not feel bad about yourself after looking in the theoretical mirror; rather, use this self-reflection to help you see where you shine and where you need to get out the polishing kit and do a little buffing.

It's time to be honest with yourself because the dating world is brutal. What are you bringing to the table? If you previously thought you were the cat's meow but now realize you have much to work on, then it stands to reason you were likely going after the unattainable mate, which is why you are single. I once went on a date in my early twenties with a guy who thought that because he was tall and handsome and had an East Coast education that women would be impressed without him having to prove anything else about himself. He generally went after beautiful, smart, intelligent women who already had successful careers, yet he had no substance. He was incredibly arrogant and relied on his pedigree, though he hadn't even capitalized on it yet. Instead, he was working an entry-level job just like the rest of the people our age were and are expected to. Had he been more humble about working hard and admitting that a fancy education doesn't always mean much in the end, his honesty would either have helped him score one of those women or he would have changed the type of women he approached by realizing that perhaps a woman also working hard in her career to prove herself would have been more his speed.

Having realistic expectations of yourself and your date are both important mind-sets to have, and, with them, you can enter the dating scene with the security of knowing you aren't wasting anyone's time, including your own—plus you will be able to handle it when feelings aren't mutual because you'll know it's not personal. As long as you've done the work to better yourself—particularly mentally and emotionally—and you're dating someone within your realm, you will know that any disinterest from a prospect is due to the fact that the other person also knows exactly what he or she wants, and it has nothing to do with you. Thank him or her for not wasting your time and move on. This type of mind-set is the only way to survive the dating world until you meet your beshert.

Julie, twenty-eight

My girlfriend Julie has been my muse since I began writing a dating advice column in 2008. She's amazing—aside from being smart and successful, she is also one of the nicest people I know and has dozens of girlfriends to attest to her loyalty—and she is also the only one in her group of girlfriends who is still single. She would make a wonderful wife and mother, but she wants it so bad it is seeping out of her pores. Because she's had such bad luck with men, she's lost hope and has stopped taking care of herself and now treats dates like job interviews, asking status-quo questions like machine-gun fire without even waiting to hear the answers. Rather than learning from the mistakes she's made, she has let the rejection get to her and now is critical and judgmental of all men. She walks into a date expecting for it to go badly, so she doesn't even take the time to dress up, doesn't care to make any type of impression at all, and yet she is surprised when the result is just as she expected—bad.

Julie needs a restart. She needs to stop dating, take a break (see Chapter 12, Breaking Up with Dating) and rewire her brain before getting back in the dating game. Julie needs to focus the positive energy that she gives to her girlfriends on herself. Just as she's been a cheerleader for all her friends—she has been a bridesmaid no less than twelve times—she needs to pull out her pompoms and do a little routine for herself. She is awesome and she is deserving, and any man would be lucky to end up with her. She needs to ingrain those statements in her head until she believes them. But she also needs to realize she has to show men why they might want to be with her. She's got to start putting the effort into her appearance as well as her mental state. Each date is unique, and it's not fair to judge your next date just because your last date sucked. Julie needs to see each first date as an opportunity and treat it like it's her last, because it very well could be.

♥ Natalie, thirty-one

Natalie began writing me asking for advice a few years ago. She was married and divorced at a young age, but even with her dramatic backstory she has no problem attracting men. Guys don't seem to care about her whirlwind romance turned short-lived marriage, nor do they care that she lives at home with her parents though she's in her thirties. But even with so many prospects, Natalie still can't seem to find someone she wants to commit to, and guys have started to see her as the fun, party girl and not as wife material. Natalie is dating with self-proclaimed baggage that only she can unload. She clearly isn't ready to get back into the dating pool, and she should probably start seeing a therapist first. Natalie learned many things about herself during her divorce, but she did not learn anything about men—she still can't tell a good guy from a player and is continuously drawn to bad boys even as she bemoans her past mistakes.

I've encouraged Natalie to achieve a greater understanding of the growing pains she has experienced and to stop calling her divorce a "failed marriage" or a "mistake," as it was simply a really expensive learning experience. As long as she grew from it, she can't regret it—those types of phrases are what your date wants to hear when you have a background like Natalie's. Then again, Natalie also needs to figure out the type of guy she wants to date and how to attract him. She needs to gain some introspection about both herself and who she is looking to ultimately end up with. Once she fully grasps the work she needs to do, she will be able to find a commitment-worthy man.

♥ Mike, thirty-three

Mike was referred to me by a mutual friend who was concerned that Mike would end up single the rest of his life if he continued to approach dating the way he had been. For starters, he is in his midthirties and says he wants to settle down and start a Jewish family, but he continuously goes for women in their early twenties who aren't Jewish. He has set unrealistic standards for women no person could match, and, when he does eventually go out on a date with a Jewish girl slightly closer to his age, he is extremely judgmental and critical. He isn't willing to compromise on one preference and even ended a date when the woman ordered "the house wine" instead of either asking him to choose a wine from the list for her or knowing about the selection herself.

I've worked with Mike on setting up his Internet dating profile, but he refuses to publish it, keeping it hidden while he peruses the women online in secret. It took a lot of persistence on my end to get him to expand his maximum age range to thirty-three—his own age! Mike thinks he is a catch, and not just for the Jewish community but for all women, yet his attitude and ego have kept him from meeting anyone of substance, regardless of religion. I wish I could set him up on a date with Bar Refaeli or another Jewish supermodel and have it end with the woman rejecting him to prove my point and help get his head in the right place. Until he truly understands a woman is not just a pretty picture displayed on a mantel, he won't find a real woman.

♥ **Lauren, forty-one**

Lauren wrote me after her divorce was final to ask for help getting back in the dating scene. She was married ten years and has two young kids and doesn't really know who she is now. Her identity has always been "wife and mother," and prior to that she was always someone's girlfriend. Aside from the fact she hasn't dated in almost fifteen years, when she was dating, she always jumped from relationship to relationship, turning what should have been rebounds into long-term commitments, never giving herself time to recover. She moved for boyfriends and gave up her career for her husband to become a stay-at-home mom. So now she is in a city without family and hasn't had any experience in the work field in nearly eight years. She's always lived out everyone else's dreams, and now it's time for her to figure out what she wants.

I've asked Lauren to take time to herself and to be a great mom as her kids adjust to separate homes. The last thing she needs is to put her claws into another man right away. She's already taken a part-time job, which is great; she is spending time with other divorcées as she learns the ropes of single parenting; and she is already toeing the idea of entering the dating pool again. Eventually, Lauren will need to make a list of what she is looking for in a man. Obviously she needs not just a husband but also a stepfather to her children. But what else does she want in a partner? I strongly suggested she look for a man who will support her in finding her identity as she moves through her forties.

Beth, forty-eight

Beth has finally accepted the fact that at forty-eight years old, she's not going to bear children and possibly may not even adopt, but she still wants to fall in love and get married and spend the rest of her life with someone. Beth may have accepted her fate, but she still has a chip on her shoulder about the fact that after twenty-five years of dating she never met her beshert and never at least took it upon herself to have kids. Beth was focused on finding a husband throughout most of her twenties and thirties until she finally realized she wasn't being herself, and, after a lot of therapy and soul-searching, Beth came out of the closet as a gay woman. Over the last ten years she has become active on the lesbian-dating scene and still hasn't found the woman she wants to fully commit to. She doesn't know if it's her that has turned off the women she has dated or if she has been waiting for the unattainable, and this confusion has turned the little chip into a big chip and has only hardened her more when it comes to dating. At this point, the chip on her shoulder is so big that it is visible to any woman who comes within view.

Beth needs to continue dating because each date she goes on increases her odds of finally meeting someone, but her attitude has got to be adjusted. Her single status can be attributed to both possibilities—women simply not being interested in her and her being too picky—so Beth needs to edit her priorities, especially because she is no longer looking for a woman to parent with but rather one to be a companion in her life. Her list of expectations needs to be chopped in half. I only wish I could have helped her before the chance of motherhood passed her by.

 ### David, sixty-one
David is my sixty-one-year-old client who was recently widowed after thirty-five years of marriage. David is extremely

good looking and is very fit, yet he has had no luck finding someone his own age who is in the same mental and physical shape as he is. He isn't interested in dating women his daughters' ages, nor is he interested in anyone lacking substance. He wants the total package, and it's not that unrealistic of him to expect to meet her because his wife was just that amazing.

Therein lies the problem though. Any woman who comes into his life is going to be compared to his wife who, now that she's passed, will always be remembered as perfect. Things weren't always so good, but that's not what is recalled now that she's no longer here. You can't compete with a dead person. That sounds harsh, but it's true, and that harshness was what David needed to hear to understand he wasn't looking to replace his wife. David is having fun, casually dating some women while looking for a partner in life.

....

Everyone is going to have different things to work on, whether it be working on yourself or working on understanding what—or rather, who—you're looking for. Hopefully by doing some honest self-reflection you have realized where you can better yourself in order to become a hot commodity. In Chapter 2, What's Your Type? you will find out how to figure out which items belong on your list of priorities in a mate and which need to fall by the wayside to help you meet people who better match your preferences.

SO YOU THINK YOU'RE READY TO DATE? TAKE THIS QUIZ TO MAKE SURE YOU KNOW WHAT YOU'RE GETTING YOURSELF INTO!

1. Have you ever asked someone you were interested in "Why are you still single?"
a. Not in those exact words
b. Yes
c. No

2. When asked "Why are you still single?" what was your response?
a. I thought I had met the right person but . . .
b. I don't know
c. I'm waiting for the right person to come along

3. What are you looking for in a partner?
a. Attraction and passion
b. Similar interests
c. Kindness and respect

4. What tops your list of "must-haves" in a partner?
a. Height
b. Successful career
c. Close with family

5. Do you reveal your income on your dating profile?
a. No, it's no one's business
b. Yes, I have nothing to hide
c. No, not until I'm in a committed relationship

6. How many emails total do you typically exchange online before going out?
a. 20
b. 10
c. 4

7. When and where is the ideal time and place for a first date?
a. Lunch during the week so you have an excuse to leave
b. Dinner on the weekend because you're worth it
c. Drinks during the week which can lead to dinner if things are going well

8. Women: Do you offer to pay on the first date? Men: Do you reject her offer?
a. No
b. Yes
c. Sometimes, if it feels like the right thing to do

9. Should you text after a first date to say you had a good time?
a. No, better to play hard to get
b. Yes, it's a great way to show excitement
c. No, I call the next day instead

10. How do you end a bad date?
a. Leave while your date is in the bathroom
b. Give a quick kiss because you think it's expected
c. Politely say thank you and nice to meet you

If you answered mostly A then you're ready . . . to crash and burn. This book needs to become your Bible, or rather, your New Jew Testament. Read it through and then take a highlighter and a red pen and then read it again and again. Dating is not a game, it's not a job interview, and it's not for people faint of heart. You need to know what your real priorities are and how to make sure you're putting your best foot forward. There are certain expectations whether we like them or not (offering to split the cost of meals and/or rejecting said offer) and you will make a better first impression by simply following the social norm.

If you answered mostly B then you're so ready that you're reeking of desperation. Roll on some antiperspirant and sit down with this book for a couple of read-throughs. No one wants to date someone who is willing to date and marry anyone. Sometimes, sticking to the social norms to the T is also detrimental because you're just going through the motions in an effort to eek out some essence of a connection upon which to build a relationship. You can be as desperate on the inside as you want, as long as the outside—including your choice of words, outfit, and facial expressions—doesn't expose you.

If you answered mostly C then you are ready to rock and roll! Welcome to the ultimate dating mind-set. You are prepared both mentally and emotionally, you have realistic expectations, and you aren't going to dissolve into depression when rejected or on a terrible date. You are able to maintain your self-respect by respecting your date whether you're hitting it off or not. You understand how to utilize Internet dating websites and how to behave on dates. Alas, you're still single, and, although you aren't desperate, you do want and need advice to help meet someone.

Chapter 2

★ WHAT'S YOUR TYPE? ►

YOU'RE NOW MENTALLY and emotionally prepared for dating but you have no idea who you want to date outside of someone whom you're attracted to and someone who is smart, funny, and nice. Those are obvious traits that nearly everyone is looking for, but what does attraction mean to you, and how smart is smart enough, and how funny is funny enough and, yes, how nice is nice enough (or how nice is too nice)? (How Jewish is Jewish enough? will be addressed in Chapter 3, Do the Jew.)

Let's start with attraction. Attraction is definitely a must, but it can grow as mutual respect and adoration grows, and conversely, it can just as quickly diminish when there's a lack of respect and adoration. Instant physical attraction is just one part of the equation. A Brandeis University study showed Jewish couples who married based on commonalities had a lower rate of divorce than non-religious couples who married after falling in love at first sight. The Jewish couples' romances grew and strengthened due to their mutually shared values, while the lust-filled couple's romance dipped and flattened as they discovered they had less and less in common.

Anthropologist Helen Fisher says biological changes can be the reason why a couple who married due to attraction-only has a higher rate of divorce because their bodies build up a tolerance to the chemicals caused by the initial feelings of love (or lust). Whether or not you believe in that philosophy, looks do eventually fade, and you will be left with only conversation and commonalities. But if you have more than just instant attraction, you can rely on what you have in common, such as Judaism, to keep you together. In addition, Jewish marriages have a lower divorce rate compared to the general American public, so if you look for a Jewish partner, you're increasing your odds of a successful marriage once again. That doesn't mean chemistry isn't important, because it is, but, if you feel at least some sense of attraction to your mate, then allow that attraction to build before you throw your hands in the air and give up.

Most people have a physical type that they are typically attracted to, whether it's a tall man or a curvaceous woman or green eyes or brown hair. Yet physical traits might not necessarily be a high priority. I've heard many stories like this one: "I never thought I'd be attracted to him in a million years, and I was swept off my feet." I know men who always dated blonds but married brunettes and I know women who insisted on only dating tall men but ended up falling deeply in love with men closer to their own height. If you could only pick one item from your attraction list to be a must-have, what would it be? I promise you, everything else will fall into place.

Speaking of must-haves, it's time to make The List of must-haves, wants, and needs. The List takes time and many steps to craft. Start thinking about what qualities you are looking for in a mate as you create your spreadsheet—and that's not a typo. Open up Excel and get typing. I encourage you to make sure you have social, mental, and emotional items on this list. Don't forget moral, behavioral, and personality characteristics. Is the person being Jewish a nonnegotiable? Do you care if he or she already has a successful career? Is the ability to cook or the love of cleaning really a big deal? Where does a person's relationship with their parents and siblings stand? Do you care if he or she likes to watch or play the same sports as you? Does he or she need to agree with you politically? Are book smarts or street smarts more important to you?

1. Title the first column in your Excel spreadsheet THE LIST, and write down every last item you can think of that you would want in your perfect partner. Don't hold back. A dozen items is too few; fifty might be too many. The List will be narrowed down soon enough, but if you already have a super short list or a super long list then that may explain why you're still single.

2. Next, title the second column VALUE, and attach point values to these items from one to ten, with one being least important and ten being most important. (More on point values in step 6.)

3. Anything that has a value less than a seven should be deleted. And don't go changing your points now that you know this! Delete, delete, delete.

4. Take a look at the items you have left. Arrange them so that they are in order by numerical value. Are the items worth seven points really that important after all? Probably not. Delete them, too.

5. Create a final cell to calculate the average of the total points. If cell B25, for example, is where you want to see your average, you might use a variation of this formula: (SUM=B2:B24/23). (In

this example, B2 is the first cell with a value and B24 is the last cell with a value, so there are twenty-three cells with values. This formula will total cells B2 through B24 and will divide that total by twenty-three, the number of cells with values.)

6. Now create a third column with the prospective partner's name as the title and go through and determine how this person fulfills each of the items in column 1. The items are worth the numerical value you gave to them, but just because you gave an item a ten doesn't mean that a prospect has to fulfill all ten points. For instance, if you prefer a Conservative Jew and that is of utmost importance to you at ten points, but the prospect is a Reform Jew, then he or she might be given, say, a seven out of ten.

7. Calculate the prospect's score by finding the average of his or her total points by using the same formula you used in step 5. If cell C25, for example, is where you want to see your average, you might use a variation of this formula: (SUM=C2:C24/23). (In this example, C2 is the first cell with a value and C24 is the last cell with a value.) Once you have the prospect's average (in cell C25, for example), divide it by the average of your VALUE column (in cell B25, for example). Then take that total, multiply it by one hundred to create a percentage, and translate that percentage into a letter grade just as though you are back in school. If the prospect doesn't earn an A—90 percent or above—then this person is simply not fulfilling enough of your wants and needs and should be deleted along with his or her column.

Below is an example of The List with a fictional prospect named Shmulik Cohen:

The List	Value	Shmulik Cohen
Jewish	10	10
Family Values	10	8
Kind	10	9
Good Conversationalist	9	8
No Drugs or Smoking	8	5
Intelligent (mixture of book smart and street smart)	10	6
Fights Fair/Knows How to Compromise	10	9
Honest	10	8
Even Tempered	9	5
Good Manners/Polite	9	7
Says What He Means and Means What He Says	9	9
Affectionate	8	8
Not Selfish	8	6
Fun and Funny	8	7
Independent	8	6
Cultured/Well-Rounded	8	7
Financially Stable Job	8	8
Has Similar Vision for the Future	8	6
AVERAGE	8.9	7.3

As you can see, Shmulik earned a B, which is not good enough to continue into a serious relationship. As much chemistry as you may have with your own Shmulik, it's not enough to build a relationship upon.

Your spreadsheet doesn't have to be completed with each date you go on, but it is really there to remind you what's important and to keep you focused when you get blindsided by lust. Having The List handy both on paper and in your mind to consult will also help you get back on the saddle after you inevitably get burned in the dating world. Once you finalize The List, try not to edit it too often. As people get hurt they tend to make changes to The List in an effort to counteract the pain they're feeling. Just because one person rejects you doesn't mean they necessarily have bad traits; it just means it wasn't the right match. You will learn more and more about who you are and what you want with each failed relationship, and you will reevaluate what love means to you, but that doesn't mean you have to change The List with each tear you shed.

Try to wait until the one-year anniversary of the date you created The List before you edit it. If after a year you realize that a few items on The List really aren't that important anymore, then you can remove them or lower their point value. At the same time, you may want to add a few items. Must-haves in your twenties are not going to be the same if you are still single in your thirties and will most definitely change if you haven't yet tied the knot in your forties. Don't lower your standards—unless of course your standards are way too strict or unrealistic to begin with.

The List will help you battle the effects of lust—that sexual chemistry makes you willing to sacrifice your standards. Everyone gets caught up in the throes of passion, especially in the beginning of hot and heavy relationships. You imagine phone conversations, make hypothetical plans, and even dream about how you will battle obstacles together. When reality hits you—that you're lusting after this person, and nothing more—you often times end up much more disappointed than you should have been because you created a more serious relationship in your mind than what you really had—and this happens even when you are the one who ends it! Use the "Chemistry Quiz" below to help separate potential loves from the obvious lusts.

CHEMISTRY QUIZ

Step #1: When you first meet someone—whether it's through online dating, a friend, or a random meeting—decide whether you get a tingly feeling in the pit of your stomach or not.

Step #2: Once you determine if that tingly feeling is there, you need to figure out what it means. Are you just on a high from meeting someone new who shows an inkling of an interest in you, or do you feel an intangible connection and an ease that you've never felt before?

Step #3: Double-check your gut reaction. Are you so desperate to meet someone you're willing to settle and compromise on your future and overlook The List? Or is the person sitting across from you your other half, the person you've been waiting for all your life, the person you can't imagine living without? This may sound like an easy step, but it's very difficult when you're blinded by the attention and affection of someone with whom you have an intense physical attraction.

Julie

Julie has such a long, strict List of preferences no man will ever be able to meet her expectations. Not only does she want someone who graduated college—which is acceptable enough—but, if he doesn't have a higher degree (MA, MD, JD, PhD, etc.), then he must have graduated with his Bachelor's within four years from a respectable university. She will only date a man who is a Conservative Jew and keeps kosher to a degree (separate plates and utensils in the home and no eating shellfish or pork, or mixing meat and milk outside the home) except for when they order carne asada fries. Julie spends time on first dates rifling off questions that pertain to these standards so much so that the date feels more like a job interview, and then she visibly judges the answer when it's not to her liking. Julie expects certain behaviors and will tune out a date almost as soon as it begins if the prospect's manners are not impeccable. The List she created goes on and on and every item is worth ten points, yet men rarely if ever will earn the full ten points in any category. I've tried to chip away at The List Julie created by pointing out that Steven Spielberg and Bill Gates were college dropouts and that if she insists on keeping Kosher on The List then she will probably have to sacrifice her monthly trip to the neighborhood Mexican drive-thru. Julie is approaching thirty, and I believe that as the big day gets closer she will begin to realize that one day in the near future she will need to thoroughly edit her List. The List in Julie's case seems to be more of a proverbial wall than any-thing else because she is so afraid to get hurt. But it is true: If she doesn't give anyone a chance because they don't meet her criteria, then she will never have a broken heart.

LOOKING FOR LOVE STATISTICS

A recent online survey conducted by Market Tools, Inc., for Match.com found that the majority of singles want and don't want the same things. More than five thousand singles in the United States over age twenty-one were asked questions about dating, and these are some of the results:

What Men Want	What Women Want
63% want someone they can trust and confide in	**84% want** to be treated with respect
57% want to be treated with respect	**77% want** someone they can trust and confide in
40% want to have physical attraction	**58% want** someone who makes them laugh
37% want someone who makes them laugh	**47% want** someone who shares the same values
36% want a woman comfortable with her own sexuality	**46% want** someone comfortable communicating wants, needs, and desires

♥ Natalie

Not long ago, Natalie met Jason at a Jewish mixer for young adults and she thought he was cute and sweet, but her interest was both piqued and dashed when she found out he had a long-distance, long-term girlfriend. But a few weeks later, Jason broke up with said girlfriend and pursued Natalie. She was incredibly flattered and believed he was what she wanted. Three months and dozens of excruciating circumstances later, Natalie understood why his previous relationship lasted so long: because the girl didn't live near Jason! Jason wanted to be with Natalie all the time and couldn't understand why Natalie would ever want to be alone or would want to hang out with her girlfriends without him. Natalie thought she wanted Jason but was more attracted to his previous unavailability than anything else. Once he became accessible (not to mention clingy), he wasn't so attractive anymore. Natalie realized Independence needed to be added to The List as soon as the time came for her to edit her spreadsheet.

♥ Mike

Mike claims he's a major romantic and says his only non-negotiable is that he wants to find a woman who is just as romantic as he is and that when they meet they will both instantly know they are beshert. I explained to Mike that timing is a huge part of finding a wife, along with knowing more about who he wants. Mike said he doesn't believe in timing and doesn't want a girl who does either. Oy *gevalt!* This guy wants to see a burning bush when he meets his beshert and he wants her to see it, too! He knows he's *meshuganneh*

about it—he told me so himself—so he wants a woman to be crazy in love alongside him. He went on to say that he was flexible about nearly everything else in life: Career, Personality, Location, even Religion, but not her Sense of Romance (I call bullshit because I know Attraction is one of Mike's highest priorities).

I appreciated his knowledge of what his standards were, but one item does not make a List. It's simply not realistic. I'm afraid by not having anything more substantial in common than being "in love" means it's only a matter of time until the relationship comes to an end. I'm also afraid being "in love" is a drug to him and once the high wears off from one woman he'll get bored and want someone else (proven by his dating history). I confessed my concerns to him, but he was adamant about his desires. Mike will likely learn the hard way.

 Lauren

Lauren never had a List typed out and saved to her hard drive because she met her now-ex-husband when she was in her midtwenties after being in multiple long-term relationships since high school. Now that she is divorced at age forty-one and in a new dating era that not only includes her being a single mother but also has elements such as online dating that she never experienced before, she has to create a List. Topping The List for Lauren is someone who is a Parent and has Similar Parenting Philosophies, or at least someone who is open to being a stepfather and understands what that role entails. Also on her List is Jewish, because she is raising a Jewish family, and Financially Stable, because

LOOKING FOR LOVE STATISTICS

Other notable stats from the Match.com study included the desire for a date to have good teeth, which anthropologist Helen Fisher says is connected to good health and hygiene. Someone with good grammar skills was the second most popular answer to the question. Here are some more results:

Dating Data

65% of singles would not date someone with credit card debt of more than $5,000

63% of men and 44% of women have had one-night stands (28% of singles have sex by the third date, 46% have sex by the sixth date)

49% of singles would date someone who lived at home with their parents

47% of singles have been involved in a "special friends" relationship

38% of singles would cancel a date because of what they found out doing online research (48% of women and 38% of men research a first date on Facebook)

36% of singles have sent a sext (sexy photo or message via text)

28% of heterosexual singles and **46% of homosexual singles** have dated someone they met online although she is not looking for someone to pay for her children's livelihood, she already experienced enough money struggles with her ex-husband.

Lauren has a few other traits that probably wouldn't have been on her List ten or fifteen years ago—Effective Communication with Similar Approaches to Expressing Your Emotions, Fighting Fair and Knowing How to Say "I'm Sorry," The Ability to Admit When You're Wrong, and, finally, Respecting Each Person's Role in the Marriage. These are all traits Lauren had never thought about when she was in her twenties and thought finding a husband was the most important thing in the world. Hindsight is 20/20. Although she would never replace her children, she does wish she had these priorities as part of her List all along. Lauren didn't know these traits were important, so she didn't seek them or demand them. Now she will.

 Beth

Beth has been in multiple long-term relationships, including some during which she lived with the prospect. She and her last girlfriend, Dana, had been together for two years and were being asked on a regular basis when they were going to get engaged. Beth had reservations. After two years, she was still unsure if Dana was the one because she felt like Dana didn't give her the amount of attention she deserved and needed. She had tried to discuss it with Dana a number of times, but nothing ever changed. Beth finally had to decide if this one thing, the lack of affection, was a make-or-break issue. For her it was. She realized Dana was not going to change and ended the relationship before she had to reject a proposal or end an engagement. Showing Signs of Affection increased in value to a 10 on The List, whereas before she met Dana, she thought an 8 was enough.

David

After losing the love of his life and with a lifetime left to live, David is now looking for someone much different than what he was looking for when he met his wife more than thirty-five years ago. Although he will never be done mourning his wife, he has decided that after five years, he is ready to seriously begin dating, and he began a List in an effort to figure out what and who he wants. Aside from someone Close in Age and Widowed or Divorced with Grown Children, he also prefers an Educated and Intelligent woman who Watches Multiple News Channels and Reads Both Fiction and Non-Fiction and Can Have Interesting and In-Depth Conversations and Debates Without It Turning into a Fight. Yes, that last one is long-winded, but it's a very important item from The List David crafted.

David wants someone to enjoy the rest of his life with, and he knows that that means the ability to hold a conversation. He also wants someone who is Fit, Active, and Can Keep Up with him as he is youthful and in great shape. David doesn't need someone to bear children with, but he does want someone who will spoil his future grandchildren as if they were her own. David doesn't feel like his List is too narrow, and he is excited to begin looking for a partner.

Even though I just instructed you to insert two formulas into your Excel spreadsheet, my hope is that The List doesn't make you feel like dating is a formula. Use The List to remind you what's important when things get too hot and heavy or when you get frustrated beyond belief by the travesties that can result from dating. Your moral compass can sometimes get skewed, and the cliche of "trust your instincts" can be upended by ego. That's when The List will be there to right you on your path.

Chapter 3

✶ DO THE JEW ➤

LET'S START OFF THIS chapter with some old school Jewish guilt: A 2001 survey published in Haaretz found the Jewish population in the United States decreased by half a million people due to an interfaith marriage rate of 50 percent. So do you want to date—and marry—a Jew? How committed to the Jew are you? Obviously you will have far less prospects, but you will also know those prospects have already been narrowed down by a commonality far more important than loving the same football team. Of course, there are many other incredibly important values that you can find in common with someone who isn't Jewish, and many successful marriages have been built upon those commonalities, and many of those interfaith marriages include a non-Jewish spouse dedicated to the support of raising a Jewish family.

Even if you grow up in a Jewish household, religion isn't likely the first thing you consider when you start dating. Your childhood fantasies don't necessarily include religion as the ruling factor in your love life. As you reach your late teens and begin dating, you probably still don't think about religion and your future when you fall in love for the first time with someone who isn't Jewish. As you go through your twenties and thirties and forties looking for your beshert, you may begin to think about whether or not you want to marry a Jew. Maybe you think religion doesn't matter and love will conquer all. Maybe you believe that all you need is love and love is all that matters and so many other clichés. Eventually, though, you may begin to rethink your priorities and realize sharing a religion is important, not because it makes life easier (which it does) but because it means you share so many other important commonalities. You may also question how important religion is to you if you don't plan to have children—without the need to pass your cultural and spiritual beliefs on to another generation, it may be that finding a Jewish partner is less a priority. But maybe it's not, too.

Your parents more than likely imagined you marrying someone Jewish, making a Jewish home, raising Jewish children, and inviting them over to share Shabbat dinner. Unfortunately your parents can in no way prepare you for the unknown and unusual difficulties Jewish dating currently presents. The pressures put on you by your doting parents (not to mention grandparents) can instead have the reverse effect. Many Jews will rebel and date outside the Jewish faith until something brings them back to the fray. For some it may be the death of a grandparent, the birth of a niece or nephew, or some other momentous life event. When someone Jewish passes away or someone is born into the Jewish faith, the family rarely has to discuss how to mourn or celebrate, respectively. Faith-based traditions and values are ingrained from birth—specifically, your Brit Milah, or baby naming. Just know that even if you find a non-Jewish partner who says he or she will support you in raising a Jewish family, it's not the same. There's something comforting about knowing the words to "I Have a Little Dreidel" and the perfect way to cook matzo breit.

Hopefully I have you convinced by now that you do want to stay committed to dating Jews. So how do you go about finding the specimens coined by Jewish mothers as their "perfect children"? (More on that in Chapter 13.) You've got to use three things: your G-D given Jewdar powers, G-D's Chosen People, and the place where you go to connect to G-D: temple. But first, who is a Jew?

ARE YOU JEW ENOUGH?

Who is a Jew and what makes you Jewish? Tradition says that if your mother is Jewish then you are Jewish, so does that mean that those with only a Jewish father but who have grown up feeling and thinking they are Jewish actually aren't? And who are we to judge? The more conservative and orthodox Jew may not be willing to marry someone who cannot prove their bloodline, while the reform and less conservative Jew may not care how you became a Jew as long as you are one. There are many types of Jews—although not all may be accepted as Jewish by others—and you have to think long and hard about what you believe makes a Jew. If someone "feels" Jewish, is that enough for you?

So are you a Jew if you weren't born Jewish but were adopted at birth by Jewish parents, and although you were not officially converted you have no other identity than that of a Jew? Conversely, are you a Jew if your biological parents are Jewish but you were adopted at birth by non-Jews and raised a non-Jew? Are you a Jew if your Jewish father agreed to raise you with no religion or in the religion

"SHIKSAS" AND "GOY TOYS"

Words to Eliminate From Our Vocabulary

Previous generations of Jews have used terms to taunt other Jews who date outside the faith. From saying "shiksas are for practice" to a Jewish young man who is dating a non-Jewish woman, to using the term "goy toy" to describing a Jewish woman who is getting "it"—dating a non-Jew—out of her system, these terms have become all too common and are all too inappropriate. Previously, the terms were used to try and shame Jews from marrying non-Jews and, as stated earlier, finishing Hitler's work. Yes, the Jewish population is being affected by the rising numbers of interfaith dating, but that cannot be blamed solely on the non-Jew in the relationship. It's simply not fair.

The most recent generation of Jews often uses these terms more loosely, more in jest, but it is nonetheless still reverse anti-Semitism, and usually it is stemming from a place of jealousy and insecurity. Just as Jewish women don't want to be called JAPs (Jewish American Princesses) and Jewish men don't want to be seen as bank accounts and doormats, we need to stop using and accepting any of these terms and other like-minded words and phrases.

of your non-Jewish mother but yet you always felt a connection to your father's heritage? Are you a Jew if you can trace your lineage back for generations yet you rarely if ever practice Judaism, attend synagogue, or observe holidays?

Jews come in every form and in every color, and it's not our place to judge someone for how Jewish they are or are not. You have to decide what kind of Jew you are and what kind of Jew you want as a partner. Do you care if a Rabbi cares if you're Jewish, or is it more important that your spouse accepts your heritage? There is every kind of Jew on Jewish dating websites and at Jewish mixers, and there are even non-Jews online seeking Jewish spouses. Decide what spectrum of Jewishness (or non-Jewishness) you want, and don't worry about who else is out there.

JEWDAR

Jewdar allows you to sniff out Jews in a public setting like a detective on a hot trail. When you're at a bar or a party or even at a coffee shop, it's not always polite to come straight out and ask someone if he or she is Jewish; in fact, it's downright awkward. Instead, use your instincts and resort to asking subtle questions or making sly comments that will hopefully solve the mystery and let you know if this person is dating material or not. Some people stand out from the crowd as being an obvious Yid, but others need some snooping.

Let's say you're at a sports bar during a major sporting event such as Super Bowl Sunday, and a gorgeous brunette approaches you. None of the stereotypical Jewish physical characteristics are giving you any clues, so try asking a subtle question that is sports-related: "Did you pray for a Patriots win this morning?" Being that it is Sunday, the answer should be a dead giveaway. She will either say she indeed went to church that morning and added the Pats to her prayers, or she will say she skipped temple this week but she sure hopes the Pats lose, or she will say she doesn't pray but will reference what religion she was raised and what she currently believes in.

Throwing in some Yiddish phrases here and there is another way to see if someone is a tribe member. If the prospect picks up on the sly and most likely witty comments you dish out, then you have your answer. If you're at a bar and a guy is talking to you and you just can't seem to pick up on his religion, then slip in an "oy vey" when two waitresses nearly collide. Add a "la'breut" when someone sneezes. Toast "l'chaim" when the guy buys you a drink. Even a flirty "that's *mishegas*" will work. If he looks at you helplessly, then you have your answer. If he adds his own Yiddish phrase to the mix then you can breathe a sigh of relief and continue getting to know him.

JEWISH GEOGRAPHY

Jewish Geography is a great way to utilize fellow tribe members because the Jewish community is small. It's even smaller when you're dating. So everyone knows someone within six degrees . . . and probably less. Chances are you'll see the same people online, at Jewish mixers, and working out at the JCC. If you happen to run into someone you've never seen before, odds are he or she is the friend or relative of someone you've already dated or that your friend or relative has already dated him or her. The Jewish dating world can quickly become incestuous. For the most part, it's perfectly acceptable to date a former lover's friend or a friend's former lover because without such acceptance there would be no one left. There are exceptions to this of course: It depends how serious the relationship was and if it ended badly. Otherwise, go for it!

And when you meet someone you've never seen before then it should be, pardon the pun, "relatively" easy to find a connection to him or her. If it's not a neighbor of your parent's friend, then it's the college roommate of your former Torah school classmate or it's the cousin of your best friend's childhood friend. There is a connection somewhere. And when the date doesn't go as planned, then figure out which of your single friend's would match up better and make a *shidduch.* Jewish Geography needs to be used to your advantage, but you need to return the favor as well.

TEMPLE TEMPTATION

Finally, the synagogue is the obvious go-to for meeting Jewish singles. It's probably not going to happen on a random Friday night, so aim for the High Holy Day (HHD) services, the one time of the year when everyone, and I mean everyone, shows up. Temple is a great place to meet someone because you know right away the person is family-oriented and religious, at least to some degree. I don't mean to be disrespectful of Judaism, but Rosh Hashanah can be a more important day to singles than couples. Kol Nidre is like an added Jewish singles mixer on the community calendar except you're all dressed in suits instead of little black dresses and untucked button-downs with jeans. A large temple can mean seeing your Jewish Internet dating matches live and in person. Get the most out of the Jewish New Year and the Day of Atonement as possible: whether that means praying, meditating, meeting your special someone, or all three. Trust me, your Rabbi will be proud and honored to hear a new couple met when they went outside for some fresh air during his thirty-minutes-too-long sermon.

It's easy to spot the singles in the crowd. New couples sit together with their heads touching, whispering in each other's ears, holding hands during breaks, and looking smug in their coupledom. Meanwhile, singles are the ones twisting and turning, craning their necks to scan the crowd looking for the other young adults sitting wedged between their doting grandparents and nosy parents.

Grandmothers will call attention to the young gentlemen whom they think are handsome, and unfortunately their hearing loss means subtlety gives way to sheer embarrassment as they ask in their loud whispers, "Do you think he's cute, Dear?" or "Maybe he's single, Honey?" Jewish mothers, the ever-so-blunt gawkers who don't know how to look without staring, will point—with their pointer fingers—at the single sons of their friends sitting in the congregation. What they never seemed to catch on to is that singles have their own routines down.

Singles check out the crowd, make eye contact when possible, and then brush the hair out of their eyes or scratch their heads with their left hands so that any hopefuls might be adept enough to catch the fact that the ring finger is bare. Bathroom breaks are timed so that as many young singles as possible will follow the lead and get up to go outside at the same time to mingle without being disrespectful to the actual service underway.

After services are over, it is time to really get to work. This is the time to stand up straight, smile, and let your family members pimp you out. Jewish mothers are great at this. Ask them if they know the mother of the guy or gal you think is cute and single, and she'll go up to say hello and then you can follow behind to meet

DID JEW KNOW?

There are the attractive celebrities who most of us know are Jewish, such as Natalie Portman, Mila Kunis, Jake Gyllenhaal, and Adam Sandler. Then there are the celebrities who we rightly assume are Jewish based on our Jewdar (because of their last names or their "look"), such as Jason Segel, Sarah Jessica Parker, Adam Levine, and Debra Messing. Then there are those who tend to fly under the radar, such as:

Jewish Women	Jewish Men
Ellen Barkin	Justin Bartha
Emmanuelle Chriqui	Jack Black
Katie Couric	Zach Braff
Chelsea Handler	Robert Downey Jr.
Scarlett Johansson	Jon Favreau
Lea Michele	James Franco
Marilyn Monroe	Sean Penn
Pink	Joaquin Phoenix
Maya Rudolph	Michael Vartan
Jamie-Lynn Sigler	Noah Wyle

the intended. Chances are your mother's friends, who tell you time and again they wish you were their daughter- or son-in-law, can also be used to make introductions under the guise of being social and amicable.

 ## Julie

Julie is active in many Jewish organizations including politics. A few years ago, she met a guy at one organization's national conference in Washington, D.C., and quickly discovered her own sister and his best friend dated in college. That connection didn't bother them, and in fact it was kind of cute! It wasn't until a few weeks later while playing Jewish Geography they found out she had previously dated his sister's best friend's brother. It may seem distant enough a relation, but it was enough to skew his view of her. Apparently the kind of woman who would date his sister's best friend's brother isn't the same type of woman he sees himself with. Confusing, but yet still credible in a twisted sort of way.

This is how Jewish Geography can bite you in the tushy. It has helped Julie avoid players as she had heard their names through the grapevine from other girlfriend's negative experiences, but it has also hurt her when she prejudged someone without giving him a chance first. Just because someone is considered a jerk on a date that didn't go well with one friend doesn't mean he's going to be a jerk with you.

♥ Natalie

While Natalie was dating Jason, she got the flu. So Jason, the guy who later gave her the heebie-jeebies, drove nearly an hour out of his way to stop at her favorite deli, bought her a quart of Jewish penicillin (chicken noodle soup), left it on her doorstep, and then texted her to check her front door. He didn't even ring the doorbell because he didn't want to wake her up—and he also knew she would be embarrassed to answer the door in her slept-in robe, unwashed hair, and red, runny nose. He brought her the soup voluntarily, without telling or asking her, without any fanfare. It was the perfect declaration of his feelings for her, and, when she called to tell me what he had done, I could hear her beaming through the phlegm. Of course, this relationship didn't make it to the chuppah, but nonetheless it substantiated Natalie's dedication to dating only Jews.

♥ Mike

Mike, in all his pompous glory, likes to use his Jewdar to impress women. When his Jewdar spots an attractive Jewish woman at a bar, he will play a game. He will approach her and turn off all of his own Jewish tendencies while he flirts. After spending some time reeling the woman in and having her begin to wonder if Mike is worth her time, he will ask her, "Are you Jewish?" When she answers yes, Mike will smile proudly while exclaiming that he, too, is Jewish! He will then say how excited he is because he never meets an attractive Jewish girl out on the town. The woman will no doubt be thoroughly impressed.

That is, until his ploy eventually caught up with him. The last woman this line worked on turned the table right back on him when she asked, "If you're from around here and you're Jewish, then how come I've never seen you before?" and when he answered truthfully, saying, "I think Jewish mixers and Jewish dating websites are lame," she was totally turned off. She asked him, "If you want to meet a Jewish girl so badly, then why are you wasting your time barhopping?" Mike was stunned and realized he had to get rid of this approach as it made him look like a player to any woman with half a brain—and he wants both halves! He also had to rethink expressing his negative opinions of Jewish mixers—possibly by actually attending one and admitting that he has a hidden profile on JDate.

 ## Lauren

Lauren is active in the Jewish community, and her ex-husband was as well. So not only does everyone know her but they also know her situation. Jewish Geography is not necessarily in her favor here as she is preceded by her divorce story before a guy can get to know her if they meet at a Jewish fundraiser or through mutual friends. She's then put in a position of having to justify her divorce or prove the man wrong about what he may have heard or what assumptions he may have made. Then again, Jewish Geography has now weeded out bad options, because any man who makes Lauren feel this way is not the man for her.

Lauren doesn't need to be persuaded to date Jews because it is one of her priorities. Lauren has two young children and is raising a Jewish family and wants a man who also has Judaism as one of his top priorities. Lauren is spending some time getting to know herself and figuring out who she is and what she wants, but she sees Jewish dating websites in her future. That way, she can take her time, keep control of what information she reveals, and possibly find men who she may not already know.

Beth

Though Beth has accepted the fact that she's not going to have children, she still isn't sure how she feels about dating non-Jews. Even though she won't be procreating or parenting with what she hopes is a future wife, she feels a bond with members of the tribe. Beth has met non-Jews with whom she had intense chemistry but with whom there was also a missing element that couldn't be replaced with any other amount of commonalities.

Beth is grappling with this though. At what point does she give up one of her nonnegotiables for the sake of meeting someone she could spend the rest of her life with? Does her spouse need to be Jewish to observe Shabbat or attend HHD services or celebrate Hanukkah? Does her spouse need to be Jewish to support her when there's a death in the family? Does her spouse need to be Jewish to dance the hora at weddings? Beth says yes to all these questions but still wonders if it's a necessity.

David

After raising a family with his Jewish wife and now looking

forward to being a grandfather, David isn't sure his partner for the next thirty years needs to be Jewish. He celebrates all the holidays and has great pride that his daughters all are either married to or dating Jews, but he doesn't know if he needs to have a Jewish partner anymore. David has Jewish on his List, but it has the fewest points attached to it.

David dated non-Jews before he got married and always felt something was missing. And recently he's been hit on by quite a few younger women who weren't Jewish but also didn't have enough substance at their age to make a relationship with them worth his time or energy. Their religion wasn't the issue in those cases.

Chapter 4

✴ LET'S GET THIS ➤ PARTY STARTED

YOU NOW KNOW YOU'RE READY to date, and you've figured out what you want, who you want to go for, and if he or she has to be Jewish, so let's get to dating! There are so many ways to meet people nowadays that it's more of a challenge to not meet someone if you're single and putting yourself out there. Between bars, the Internet, setups, and random encounters, you must know how to market yourself so that you are putting your best foot forward in every situation. Infamous party girl Tara Reid (who is not a Jew) once said about her nights out on the town, "You're not going to meet anyone sitting at home alone on your couch." Not that I'm advising you to take advice from the *American Pie* actress, but she has a point: You must be proactive when it comes to dating.

Chapter 5, No More Hating on Internet Dating, will cover everything online, but let's start here with what you can do to increase your odds when you're trying to meet someone in person. At times it might feel impossible to meet a nice, single Jew at a bar because the odds are not in your favor ... but the more you go out, the better your odds get. Make a pact with yourself to go out twice a week, whether it's to a Jewish mixer, a networking event, happy hour, a celebration, or just because. You may wonder about the quality of the person you would meet at a bar and, of course, inversely, if they would take you seriously as a prospect after meeting you at a bar. But look at it this way: You're both at the bar for a reason, whether it's for a friend's birthday party or a ladies, or guys, night out or to celebrate a coworker's promotion. You're both there, so it can't be too bad, can it?

Get involved in Jewish life. Start going to Jewish events that are age appropriate. If you are pushing fifty, don't go to a young-adult event; find the groups that are geared toward you. Your local JCC and Jewish Federation have loads of information, and they'll gladly help find you the appropriate contact and details. From volunteers to single parents to young professionals to senior citizens there truly is a Jewish group for everyone. Every group has an event during every major Jewish holiday, and those are the "must go" events because the attendance is highest. The weekly or monthly happy hours are smaller and more intimate, but you also may see the same faces over and over again, so try to space those out and mix them up with other events.

Mainstream hobby groups are also a great way to meet someone. Odds are there will be a few Jews there, and, even if they're not a romantic match, they can become new friends who have other Jewish single friends to introduce you to. If you like hiking, jogging, reading, soccer, crafts, music, or anything else, find a group and do the things you love to do with other people.

Whether it is a singles mixer or a trip to the grocery store, a night out with your friends at a club or working out at the gym, you need to be dressed to impress at all times. If you know you're going to happy hour after work, then wear clothes that are suited to go from day to night—meaning, make sure your shirt underneath your jacket is clean and flattering. Throw some toiletries in your briefcase or purse so you can freshen up before you head out: Brush your teeth, run a comb through your hair, and reapply your deodorant and makeup. Don't think a quick glance in the mirror is enough; take the time to make sure you look good. Get rid of the threadbare, shlumpy gray T-shirt and baggy sweatpants you throw on for running errands or working out and upgrade. It is a pain in the *tuchus* to think about dressing up just to go sweat that tuchus off, but it will be well worth it when you meet someone along the way.

MIXERS

If you know you're going to a singles mixer after work, then don't stop at freshening up. Try to get home to take a quick shower and change your clothes, but, if there's no time to do that, bring a change of clothes with you to work, including shoes. You have been sitting at a desk in the same clothes you put on at seven o'clock that morning, a full twelve hours before attending an event where you hope to meet your beshert. I repeat, DO NOT go to a singles event after work without changing your clothes first. You want to look put together, smell fresh, and let interested parties know you took the time to get ready for the event. Finding love is important to you, so make it a priority to schedule some time in your day to look good in the evening. Once you get to the event, remember this one little detail (it always gets me): that's penmanship on name tags. If your name tag wasn't printed out, then slow down and take the time to print your name in all caps. If you have to write something about yourself on the sticker, then keep to the caps and try to think of something interesting yet cutesy. If there's someone at the check-in, then ask him or her to do a once-over for you. Do you need to button or unbutton one more button of your collar? Do you have anything in your teeth? Should you leave your shirt tucked or untucked? Use every opening to better yourself to your benefit.

WEDDINGS

Weddings are another great opportunity to meet people. When you're single at a wedding you spend the cocktail hour wondering who else has the same number on their place card, and once you get to your table it's a risk to place your card down to save your seat before knowing who else will be joining you. Are you going to be stuck next to the guy with the halitosis or the girl who won't stop jabbering or the empty seat of the person who decided not to show up . . . and which is worse?

Sure, it can be the pits to be sitting at the singles table, but put on your best dancing shoes and show up ready to celebrate someone else's good fortune at finding love. You never know who may be stuck at that table with you even though you're probably wondering, *If these other singles are so great, then why haven't the newlyweds set us up before?* but try to look past that and scope out the possibilities. Chances are only half the people at the table are, well, "normal." Hopefully there's not a seating chart and you can move around freely, but if there is assigned seating just pretend to be long-lost camp friends with the more sane singles and ask the distant cousin whom the bride always describes as "odd" to switch with you. And if that's not possible, then make a subtle escape plan to the bar with the other "normals," where you can help the new couple reach their bar tab minimum while you get loosened up and ready to hit the parquet for the Hava Nagila and Electric Slide. Enjoy yourself. The last thing people are attracted to is someone who lets the situation affect their attitude, especially at what is supposed to be a *simcha,* or joyous occasion.

A few last tips about weddings. First: Keep it classy. That means, dress respectfully yet sexy. It also means don't get wasted or sneak out of the wedding with a bridesmaid or a groomsman and think no one noticed, because everyone was watching. Second: Be a happy and willing participant. Help lift your friend up in the chair and dance in circles until you're dizzy. Clap and laugh during the cake-cutting when the bride and groom smash cake in each other's faces. Be there to at least pretend to catch the bouquet or garter. Weddings can be really fun if you don't allow them to become some sort of pity party about you still being single but your friend finding someone. Play Jewish Geography during dinner, and hopefully at the end of the night you'll leave with a phone number and can ask the newlyweds for their blessing before the honeymoon, plus get feedback from any other mutual friends you discover.

LADIES, LISTEN UP!

Makeup is an art, but not everyone is an artist. And though makeup is not for everyone, many women who do wear it end up being either over–made-up or under–made-up. I'm a fan of the natural look—applying a minimal to medium amount of makeup before you walk out the door can amplify your best features but not dominate your face. I always figure prospects want to see your true face and don't want to be surprised when the lights in the bar turn on. If you're uncomfortable using makeup but are interested in knowing more about it, you can go to a cosmetics counter at a high-end department store and learn from the pros.

Most important: Be yourself, and that means feeling confident and pretty, not primped and fake. If you feel more confident wearing a lot of makeup or no makeup at all, then do so. At the end of the day you need to feel comfortable in your skin, and no amount of makeup advice is going to replace your own feeling of self-worth. Singles are attracted to confidence.

LOOK ME IN THE EYES

Eye contact is something else you need to be cognizant of; you may even want to practice before going to mixers or on dates. Eye contact, whether it's with a boss, a coworker, a family member, a friend, or a prospective date, shows you're confident, but, more important, it shows you respect who you are talking to and want to hear what they are saying just as much as you want them to hear what you have to say.

Eye contact is probably the most important form of non-verbal communication. Eye contact is the first form of flirting, so why would you give it up once you're having a conversation? Eye contact—or lack thereof—is a social cue, so make sure you know what message you want to send before you start roving. Simply put: Maintaining eye contact lets the person know you're interested, but a wandering eye means exactly the opposite. It's preferable to just excuse yourself and walk away rather than be rude by constantly looking over someone's shoulder. You don't want anyone to have to say, "Um, yeah, my eyes are over here."

I can't remember the amount of times I wanted to (or actually did) tell a guy that. Ladies can expect a man to gaze at her cleavage or her legs or whatever skin is exposed. But what is worse is when a guy is looking past you. I remember one specific guy who was scanning the crowd behind me all the time, and I kept doing the bob and weave to keep myself in his line of sight. It got to the point where I wasn't even interested in the guy anymore but was actually enjoying watching him sidestep me. What or who was he looking at? I didn't bother turning around to look because I didn't care. He wasn't looking at me and making eye contact, and that was all that mattered. Eye contact lets someone know that you're interested. Your follow-up questions and witty comments mean diddly-squat to me if you're not looking at me when you say it.

ATTITUDE IS EVERYTHING

Next, make sure your attitude is adjusted for meeting potential prospects. If you had a shitty day at work, then maybe don't go out if you can't shake it off. Or call a friend on the way to the bar or restaurant to vent so that by the time you arrive, you have the drama out of your system. Your body language also needs to reflect your positive attitude: Don't cross your arms across your chest or put your hands on your hips; stand up straight and put a smile on your face. The saying "look good, feel good" means once you've got your clothes, face, and hair right, you'll feel better and have more confidence, and that will shine through to the people around you. A study shows that when you smile, your brain releases endorphins and sends signals to other parts of your body so that you actually start to feel happy no matter how you felt before you started smiling. So if you're not so pleased to find yourself at a singles mixer,

SMILE. You'll start to feel better, and, not only will you attract people, but you will also start to see others smiling because happiness is contagious. And nobody wants to talk to someone with a frown on his or her face, no matter how pretty that face is!

The newly coined phenomenon "Bitchy Resting Face" is what I'm talking about here. If you suffer from Bitchy Resting Face, then when you are relaxed and expressionless, everyone thinks that you're pissed off or unhappy. Plastic surgeons say it happens when the corners of your lips or your eyebrows start to droop. One of my girlfriends who I used to go out with a lot was a gorgeous girl who would sit on a barstool or in a booth completely expressionless. Guys would still come up to her because she was beautiful, but the first thing they would say was, "Smile, you look like a bitch," or they would come up to me and ask why I was hanging out with such a bitch. They didn't know her and they didn't want to take the time to get to know her because her lack of facial expression was a huge turn off. She tended to do this on purpose because she didn't want to be bothered by 99 percent of the men who would have otherwise approached her, but what if that isn't your intention? The plastic surgeons who have commented on BRF say that you can train yourself to smile even when your face is relaxed so that rather than your mouth turning downward, it starts to curl up, which makes you appear more approachable.

Putting yourself out there means you have to learn to self-promote. It's difficult for people—well, humble people—to speak highly about themselves, but in dating you need to be able to brag about yourself. It will be awkward at first, but, as long as it's presented in a tasteful way, you will get used to it. When you're modest it can be difficult to discuss how great, fabulous, smart, funny, nice, and successful you are. But you have to.

 HOW TO WOO A JEW

MAKE ME A MATCH

What's great about a matchmaker, or a *Shadchan,* is that he or she can talk you up on your behalf. The Shadchan (as in someone who makes a *shidduch,* or sets you up with someone, not to be confused with a Yenta, or meddler, although the two are often mistakenly used interchangeably) is a person who performs a service seeped in Jewish tradition from the beginning of time and read about in the Torah. The matchmaker would measure a family's background and reputation and the daughter's devotion to Torah as well as her physical looks, and he or she would find appropriately suited men from appropriately suited families. Once the parents spoke to each other and approved the union, only then would the couple meet, get to know each other, and decide if they wanted to spend any further time together. These Shadchans were paid upon creating a successful union and were sometimes even paid double if the families were extremely satisfied (conversely, a Shadchan who failed time after time was often banned from matchmaking).

Nowadays, a matchmaker can be hired from an online network or can be found through your local Rabbi or a referral. Whether you hire a Shadchan or find someone who's probably more of a Yenta but wants to help you find love via their nosy network, they will ask you questions similar to those from an Internet dating questionnaire: Who are you, what are you looking for, what is your relationship history and what have you learned from it, and what is your idea of the perfect first date? The "Who are you?" question is a difficult one to answer, but be honest and then let the Shadchan do the promoting for you. Answering all of these questions helps get you mentally prepared and measures your maturity and readiness to take the next step. If you're too abashed to answer, then you may not be ready, so go back and reread Chapter 1.

Julie

Julie is in a predicament. She is in yet another girlfriend's wedding, and it's another destination wedding, and she has been invited to bring a date, again. But "invited" is too polite a word. She is being forced to bring a date. The bride is being adamant about the situation: Apparently she needs an even number of people at the head banquet-style table so it's balanced. Unfortunately, Julie isn't dating anyone seriously right now, and the bride is surprisingly okay with Julie bringing a complete stranger or a platonic friend or even her brother to the wedding just as long as she brings someone to complete her seating chart. Julie doesn't know what to do. The bride is her former college roommate, who is Catholic and lives across the country, so Julie wasn't even counting on meeting someone at the wedding, but, yet, she was just fine going alone and being a good friend. Now she will probably end up asking one of her good guy friends to accompany her although she feels bad asking someone to pony up the funds for such a formal wedding when they are not romantically involved.

 ## Natalie

Natalie has been going out and she does great at mixers even though she's not quite sure she's ready for a relationship yet. In fact, her disinterest is probably what attracts men to her. Natalie is putting herself out there a little too much considering that she isn't sure how she feels about commitment at this point. People will get too used to seeing her and won't know when she is ready and serious about finding someone when that time comes. She can be seen at every Jewish event, every mixer, every party, and online as well. Natalie knows what to do to put herself out there, and she gets hit on, but she needs to reel it in until she is absolutely sure she is ready to start dating seriously. In the meantime, she has made a great wingwoman, as her girlfriends who would otherwise be wallflowers are front and center socializing with Natalie and getting some much-needed and much-deserved attention as well.

 ## Mike

Mike is known for constantly looking over, around, and even through the heads of whomever he is talking to, whether it be a friend or a good-looking single gal. When our mutual friend introduced us, he even scanned the room while talking to me, and here I was trying to get to know him so I could set him up! I was definitely not impressed. What Mike doesn't know is that everyone notices it—friends and potential lovers—and finds it obnoxious. I'm embarrassed on his behalf by the number of people who have made this observation to our mutual friends. With this simple action he makes people feel unimportant and obsolete. If friends of friends like me feel insulted by it, then single girls are definitely going to be turned off!

Lauren

After nearly fifteen years of being off the market, not to mention all of the long-term relationships she was in before she was married, Lauren has no idea how to self-promote nor where to go to do so, for that matter. Lauren is warming up to the idea of online dating, but in the meantime she is going out here and there with some friends. Lauren doesn't know how to dress to attract attention as she hasn't had to do so for a long time, and she doesn't know how to talk about herself in a positive way without bringing up her ex-husband or her children. Lauren needs her girlfriends to step in and give her a Single Mommy Makeover, show her how sexy she is, and remind her of the fabulous things about her that have nothing to do with her familial roles. Of course she should be proud of being a great mother, but she also needs to be proud of being a great friend, a smart woman, a selfless volunteer, and so on. She must figure out how to identify with something other than wife and mom.

Beth

Beth allows her current attitude to be written all over her face and body. She is either happy and relaxed and there-fore smiling with her arms swinging by her sides, or she is uptight and pissy with her face set in a grimace and her arms crossed and her shoulders hunched. When it's the latter, it appears Beth doesn't want to be wherever it is she is. If she's at a Jewish singles mixer then she comes across as one of those people whose parents paid for her ticket and forced her to attend the event, even if that's not the case. On top of all that, she will stand by the wall at these events or wander aimlessly and not give off any semblance of someone inter-ested in meeting prospects. Beth ought to stay home if she's not in the mood, or have a meditation-type of routine ready in order to get her in the mood for going out.

David

David merely has to go in public with his daughters, sans wedding ring, to get attention from women. He's good looking and he's confident, and since he's mature yet youthful he gets women of all ages hitting on him. David is overwhelmed by the attention and needs help figuring out how to weed through the masses to find a woman of substance. David needs to contact other widows in his community as well as look in the local Jewish magazine to find out where the singles his age are meeting. David would do well with a matchmaker who will be able to ask women the right questions to see if any are a good match for David. Speed-dating and other gimmicky mixers are probably not going to benefit David, who needs more one-on-one time to see if a woman can keep him mentally engaged. Having friends from his generation throw dinner parties with singles their age would be the best way for David to get his dating life jump-started.

Chapter 5

⬥ NO MORE HATING ON ➤ INTERNET DATING

GRAB SOME SNACKS AND get comfortable because we are in for a long ride. Internet dating is here to stay, and, if you're single and not online yet, then you're missing out on thousands and thousands of prospects. Actually, 40 million people are on online dating websites. At some point every single Jew ponders the option of creating a JDate account. And every Jewish mother hoping for a grandchild will offer to pay the membership fee. Take up your meddling mother's offer and get busy, because there are thousands of eligible Jews out there just waiting to find their beshert.

There are many websites to choose from, and many can fit your needs, whether you want one specifically for Jews, specifically for more religious Jews, a more mainstream website, a free website, or anything else. You can choose to start with one website and branch out from there if you want to, or you can sign up for multiple sites and figure out which is best for you after trying them for a few months. If you're serious about finding your beshert, then don't waste your time with the more unconventional websites that don't ask very many questions about who you are and what you're looking for in a partner, and avoid websites that have pictures and profiles of people who look like models—they probably are. Some websites pay to use models' photos to draw people in and, once you sign up, those models unsurprisingly cannot be found or have not been active on the website for months.

JDate.com is a great choice if you are looking to stay within the Jewish religion. There's also JewishMingle.com and JMatch.com if you want a matchmakers' assistance online, and there's a plethora of other sites that you'll need to vet yourself. If you're more religious, there's Frumster.com and SawYouatSinai.com as well as others that may or may not have a reputable following in the Orthodox community (if you are going this route, ask a few fellow religious singles for their recommendations to lead you to the best websites).

And then there are the mainstream dating websites such as Match.com and eHarmony.com, which ask you your religion and also ask you if religion should be one of the priorities used in the algorithm they use to make their matches. You have to make it clear when you answer their questions that Judaism is not something you are willing to negotiate on so that you don't waste your time or anyone else's.

JDATE: MEMBERSHIP

Let's say you've chosen JDate to begin your foray into Internet dating. You will have a choice of a free membership—one with certain restrictions—or a one-month, three-month, or six-month membership. The more months you commit to, the less you will pay per month. If you buy a one-month membership, you may end up buying another one-month membership, and then another, and then another, and you may find yourself being on JDate for six months or more! Or, you can shell out the bucks (hint: call Mom) for the six-month deal and end up not needing it after four months. You don't have to pay until you complete your profile. Don't feel any pressure to activate your account until your profile is completed, looked at again with fresh eyes, and then reviewed by a trusted confidant.

JDATE: PROFILE NAME

What JDate will make you do first is create a profile name. Do not, DO NOT, use the number combination they automatically assign to you. This is the first way to show that you haven't put in the full effort. On JDate, your real name is inconsequential; your profile name is essential. The first thing people see is your profile name, even before they see your photo (depending on their view settings). If your first impression is your only impression, make it the best impression possible. Take the time to spiff up your profile name.

With hundreds of thousands of singles currently on JDate, it has become increasingly difficult to invent an original name. But it's not impossible. Don't simply add a jumble of letters and numbers to the end of your name. Nouns and adjectives work best. Between your name (first, middle, or last), your hometown or current town, your school (undergrad, law school, medical school, the acronym, or even the mascot), your profession, your hobbies, and descriptions of your appearance, there are plenty of combinations that will both be unique and reflect something about you. Here are some great examples: TallJew4U, HarvardShopaholic, MITballer,

JennaLovesLaw, DrJordantheJew. Don't use your current age because there is a chance you will still be on JDate on your next birthday, and maybe even the birthday after that, so it will become obsolete. Play with words, have fun, be creative, and think about what kinds of profile names you would or wouldn't click on and then apply those considerations to your name.

You can also be funny. The more popular profile names are the ones that elicit a smile. As Jews, we have plenty of inside jokes that we can exploit, like these names do: ShortButSweet, JewishMothersDream, NotAGentile, Ready2BreakGlass, NotAnOrdinaryJew. My first JDate name was "niceJAP4u." The term Jewish American Princess has a negative connotation, as I described in Chapter 3, but I figured if a guy could see the humor in it, then he was for me. Plus, in the About Me section of the profile, I would have the opportunity to explain what my profile name meant to me.

What's not a good idea is to use too much personal information as your profile name. You can never be too safe when it comes to identity theft, so stay away from using your first and last name together. Remember: For the most part, JDate profiles can be viewed by anyone, not just paying members. Focus on making up a clever and unique profile name that will catch the attention of those you hope to attract. If your funny bone is on vacation, don't worry; just try to let your personality come through in the allotted number of characters and don't forget that everyone on JDate went through the same agonizing process.

JDATE: PHOTOS

Now you have to choose photos. There are so many mistakes made in this category it could be an entire chapter itself. You now know others see you as 20 percent more attractive than you see yourself, so it would make sense to enlist a trusted friend or relative to help you choose—or even take—your photos. Since the prospects will be strangers looking at your photos, they won't know your personality to help get that extra 20 percent boost automatically, which is why having someone who will tell you the ugly truth is imperative to this process. You think you look good in those oversize sunglasses or that straight-rimmed cap? Think again.

JDate now gives you the option to use twelve photos, which is quite a lot. I think a happy medium of six is plenty enough to show consistency in your look. Follow the five F's for photos:

Face

The first photo is considered your main profile photo. This photo must be a clear close-up—no hats, no sunglasses, no one else in the photo. They say the eyes are the window to the soul, so make sure your eyes are clear and visible. A smile can light up your face, so make sure the photo is a happy one. And don't crop out your neck! Floating heads are never attractive.

Full Body

The second photo needs to be full body. Don't worry about your size because everyone has a type; owning your body shape and exuding confidence will go much further than not answering the body style questions and never showing yourself below the neck. That is suspicious to everyone. You don't need to be wearing a bathing suit or even showing a lot of skin, but you should feature at least one photo of you from head to toe.

Fun

Use that Halloween photo, beach photo, party photo, or other photo showing you having fun for your third picture. This is not the place for your corporate business photo or the extra copies of your passport photo. Uptight is downright wrong for JDate. This photo should feature you acting goofy or participating in a sport or hobby. It can be a photo of you on vacation jumping off a pier into the ocean or pretending to hold the Leaning Tower of Pisa in your hand or kissing a statue. Show your personality and your fun and adventurous side.

Family and Friends

The fourth photo should be with people you love, either your friends or family. JDate will use their magic powers to identify you and zoom in on you for the thumbnail, and when a prospect clicks on the photo it will reveal the rest of the people in picture. Make sure you refer to the people in your photo in the description or later on in your About Me section so people don't think your brother is your ex-boyfriend or your niece is your daughter. If you have a great circle of friends or are close to your family, then simply say so.

Final Photos

That's four of the recommended six. Use the final two options to solidify your look. The worst thing is inconsistency. I've seen so many profile pictures where one photo shows tan skin, the other fair, one photo shows short hair, the other long, one photo shows the person looking younger, the other much older. If you have a super awesome amazing photo of yourself wearing sunglasses OR a hat (not both), then use it as the fifth or sixth to complement the preceding four. Make sure your photos are not more than one year old. If you recently cut or colored your hair, then you can use older photos as one of the last two, but the first four need to show how you look today. Pictures shouldn't be taken from too far away and shouldn't be fuzzy. And "selfies," photos taken by yourself with your smartphone, are not for JDate. Save those for when you're in a relationship. Or not. We are adults after all; leave the selfies to the Instagram-obsessed teenagers.

I'm often employed by men and women alike to perform JDate Extreme Profile Makeovers, and time and time again I am stunned when I scan through profile photos. One girl had a total of eight photos, so I thought, great, we can see if her looks are consistent. Well, they were consistent in that she was wearing sunglasses in four of the photos! So half of the photos were a waste of time. The fifth photo was of her with a woman I assume is her sister, but, at first glance, you get thrown trying to figure out which girl you're supposed to be checking out. The sixth was a side profile of her kissing a statue, which shows she's fun and well traveled, but you can't see her face. It would have been fine as the sixth photo. The seventh and eighth pictures were taken from far away, so you could see her body type, but you still couldn't see her face. So out of the eight photos, only one showed her full face, but there was another woman sharing the frame. What was this girl thinking? Alas, her mistakes are not uncommon. Most profiles I see feature people looking sideways, down, or hidden by sunglasses. Then there are the guys who post photos with another woman in them, and the women who post with a guy in them. It doesn't matter if the other person is your sibling or a friend, if they are cute or not; all people see is a potential past (or current) mate in the photo with you. If you're trying to make your viewers jealous, it's not working—it's only turning them off.

Think of it this way: If you were in a bar you would look at your prospect and smile, not put on your sunglasses and turn your face to the side. The same goes for your online dating profile picture. Why bother trying to hide something if you're going to meet someday? I say put it all out there, and, if people are going to reject you, let them do so in an educated manner. That may seem harsh, but at least you know they didn't like you—or not like you—for a person you're pretending to be. Be honest: If you're bald, don't wear a hat; if your hair is curly, don't flatiron it; if you've gained weight, don't show pictures from when you were recovering from the flu after running in a marathon. Since you do plan on meeting the other person eventually—and you wouldn't be on JDate if you didn't— then they're eventually going to see for themselves how you really look. Thus, you want to look better than the pictures you post, but you definitely need to, at the very least, look like your pictures.

JDATE: IN MY OWN WORDS

Now it's time to get writing. Not everyone is good at writing or at conveying themselves on paper. It's not easy. But when it comes to JDate or any other online dating website, you don't really have a choice. Let me help you first with the basic questions, which luckily for most people are simple answers:

- What is your marital status (single, divorced, widowed)?

- Which gender are you and what gender are you seeking (woman seeking man, man seeking woman, man seeking man, woman seeking woman)?

- What is your age?

- Where do you live (city, state, country)?

- Do you have kids and do you want kids?

- How tall are you?

- What type of Jew are you (reform, traditional, conservative, etc.) and how frequently do you attend synagogue (only on High Holy Days, on Shabbat, every week, etc.)?

- What is your education level (high school, associate's degree, bachelor's degree, masters, JD/MD/other postdoctoral degree)?

- What is your occupation (entertainment, sales, marketing, education, etc.)?

- Do you smoke (yes, no, sometimes)?

For the next questions, you have to post longer answers. You don't want to repeat too much of what you answered in the questions above unless something is really relevant. You don't have to answer all the questions, but try to answer as many as possible. Some are redundant, so it makes sense to skip some (see below), but, if you only answer a few, it shows a lack of effort. Luckily, the questions you don't answer disappear—JDate doesn't post "question unanswered" in the blank. Here's what you'll have to write about:

About Me

The first few words you write here is what shows up in "list" viewing formats, which is why it is important to be aware what your first sentence is. Come up with something catchy that encourages people to click on your profile and read more. Some bad examples include: "How you doin'?" (read with the voice of Joey Tribbiani from *Friends*) and "I'm new to this" (especially when the profile is more than a year old) and "I'm loking for a sweat person" (use spell-check people! And then have a friend read it over to find any homonyms that are spelled correctly but used incorrectly).

A lot of people use the phrase "my friends would describe me as" to begin this section (this is not bad, but get more creative with it instead of using it word-for-word). It's a great way to describe yourself using positive adjectives such as kind, caring, loyal, funny, smart, passionate, and so on. And then expand upon the description by selling yourself. If you're funny, don't just say, "I have a great sense of humor" but rather, "I promise to keep you laughing all day long." If you're smart, don't say, "I'm a genius" but rather, "I've never lost at a game of chess, but I'll let you win." If you're successful, don't say, "I'm rich" but rather, "I've worked really hard and now it's time to settle down."

Try not to use clichés. Everyone might be looking to share the rest of his or her life with someone, but how can you say that in a unique way that expresses your personality? Something like, "I want to fall in love with my best friend, someone I can golf with, watch *Top Chef* with, and root for the Bruins with," shows your interests and hobbies without just listing them and conveys the same message in a stronger way. Make sure your paragraph isn't stiff or formal; this isn't a cover letter for a job interview. In fact, you need to turn up the volume an extra couple of decibels, as most people's energy gets lost online. You can't assume the reader is going to read your words in the tone you intended. One paragraph of about five sentences is plenty. If it is too long, you will lose the reader; if it is too short, they will wonder what you're trying to hide.

My Life and Ambitions

In this section, talk about what you do now and what you want to do in the future. If you're a lawyer at a corporate firm but want to go into adoption law, say so here. But if you also said the same thing in the About Me section, then either delete it there or don't answer this section. Many people write here that they desire to get married and start a family, but you can also answer that later under the My Ideal Match multiple choice questions, which will be addressed in the next section. So again, this question can be left unanswered.

A Brief History of My Life

The title says "brief" so keep it brief: I grew up in _____, with parents who have been married ____ years and ____ siblings who have blessed me with nieces and nephews. I attended college at _____ and then moved to _____ to pursue a career in _____.

 That's all it has to be.

My Perfect First Date

This one is kind of a doozy. Most people say something along these lines: "My perfect first date is dinner that never ends because the conversation flows and the chemistry is amazing and we make plans to see each other again the next day." Try to jazz it up a little bit with some local venues (a walk through the so-and-so trail, drinks and dinner at the such-and-such hole-in-the-wall yet impressive restaurant, live music at that trendy yet obscure blues club) and of course tie it up in a pretty bow with the fact that you hope the conversation continues until the sun comes up, after which you'll seal the deal with a sweet and sexy first kiss.

On Our First Date, Remind Me to Tell You the Story About . . .

This is a fun one. But remember, it says to "remind me to tell you the story," so don't go into the details here. Mention just a couple words, such as: my first and last trip to Tijuana, skydiving in Brazil, walking with the lions in South Africa, and so on. If nothing comes to mind, there are always the stories about a trip to Las Vegas (which are supposed to stay in Vegas . . .), which make for a great conversation starter.

The Things I Could Never Live Without

In this section, again, most people say the same thing. This one can be skipped, but it does show what someone's mind-set is. If you're going to answer, then the word "family" has to be first. Everyone wants someone who makes family a priority, whether it is their family of origin or their future family or their friends who are like family. After "family" then you can get fun and funny. A lot of people will write down their favorite electronics, but, if you do this, balance the list out with items that don't need batteries. Can't live without your iPhone? Fine. But then mention how you will never part with the watch your grandfather gave you before he died. Some people will also mention their favorite food or album. As long as your priorities are straight then have fun answering this question.

My Favorite Books, Movies, TV Shows, Music, and Food

These questions get asked again on the next tab of your profile in a long list of similar questions all followed by a gazillion multiple choice answers. But if "fiction" or "sushi" or "pop" isn't enough of a description for you— and it probably isn't—then go ahead and give a few answers. Most people are now answering this question in list form, but don't just go on and on and list every single book you've read or movie you've seen or TV show you've watched.

Here's an example:

Books: anything by Jonathan Franzen; anyone but J. K. Rowling

Movies: *The Breakfast Club* never gets old, and neither does *The Shawshank Redemption*. I'll watch anything but horror movies.

TV Shows: *Friends, Seinfeld, How I Met Your Mother,* and *Happy Endings*

Music: Everything really, I just love good music.

Food: The chef at my favorite hole-in-the wall sushi joint knows me and my special rolls. I could eat there multiple times a week! Just don't order a trendy California Roll in front of me, please. I'm talking REAL sushi eaten the REAL way.

The Coolest Places I've Visited

This section can be skipped. But if you said you "love to travel" in your About Me, then you ought to back that up with a list of the top four or five places you've been to. If not, this part's not imperative.

For Fun I Like to . . .

This one is another doozy. But it can be skipped. We all know you probably like to spend time with family and friends, eat good food, listen to great music, enjoy good weather, etc, etc, etc.

On Friday and Saturday Nights I Typically . . .

This question is basically asking, do you observe Shabbat on Friday and do you have a life on Saturday? It's not a very important question since you answer how religious you are in various other areas and since not many people go out clubbing every single Saturday night. Most people who do respond mention having dinner with friends at home or at a restaurant and going to see a movie, grabbing some drinks, and sometimes going dancing. Which makes this a dud of a question. It's not a super important one to spend time on.

I'm Looking for . . .

Contrarily, this is an important question that seems to get answered in a similar way by everyone. Most people say something like, "I'm looking for my best friend, a partner in life, someone whom I can share everything with, where there's a deep chemistry and attraction, and most important, mutual respect." These are definitely keywords you should use here, but be genuine to how you feel, not what you think you are expected to write. What ARE you looking for?

My Ideal Relationship

Your response to this question should be just about the same as your response to the question above. To avoid repetition, pick one, discard the other.

My Past Relationships

Ugh. I hate this question. It's so silly. What do they expect people to say, that they learned how to throw a shoe across the room? Or that they learned how to get sexually frustrated? Or that they learned what a broken heart feels like? The best way to answer this question is how most people answer it, which is usually something along the lines of, "I learned more about who I am and who I want to be in a relationship and what I want from a relationship and how to spot someone who isn't right for me. I have no regrets."

You Should Definitely Message Me if You . . .

What else are you going to say besides, "Like what you read and want to get to know more"? Although some people have come up with interesting and sometimes humorous answers along the lines of, "If you think you're my lobster" or "If you want to share a bottle of Chianti" or "If you like waking up before dawn for a bike ride." If you can't think of anything catchy, then just stick to the generic answer or don't answer at all.

Details and My Ideal Match

On the right side of the main profile page is a column with two sections: Your Details (titled "His Details" or "Her Details") is all about you, and My Ideal Match is all about what you're looking for. Let's start with what you'll see in the Details column:

- Physical Info is easy to answer, and you ought to do so truthfully. Height is easy, but there's no need to reveal your exact weight if you don't want to. If it feels more comfortable, skip that and answer Body Style instead. Definitely answer the hair color and eye color questions.

- Lifestyle offers more information about you, though you answered a lot of these questions when you first started your profile (marital status, has/wants kids, synagogue, and smoker). The rest should be completed now. In this section you'll find questions such as, Are you willing to relocate? This is an important question to answer but ,if you're not sure, then select "Not Sure." Easy enough. If you do have kids and are divorced, then what is your custody? Do you own pets? Do you keep kosher? Do you drink? What is your Activity Level? Simple enough. Don't overthink this section.

- Background asks some repetitive questions including some about your religion, education, and occupation, so there are only a few necessary questions left. You previously stated where you live, so now answer in which city/state/country you Grew Up In. What is your ethnicity and what languages do you speak? In what area of study did you focus on in college, if you went? There's also a question here for you to answer in your own words: They ask you to describe What I Do. Don't be too vague or too specific, and don't say, "I'll tell you later." People want to know what you do for a living, so tell them here. On the flip side, do not ever post what your annual income is, as it is absolutely no one's business. Politics is only an important question to answer if politics is important to you. Same goes for zodiac sign.

The My Ideal Match column is the place for you to narrow down who it is you're looking for and for prospects to see if they fit your preferences. What gender you're looking for has already been stated in your profile. Everything else needs to be completed. Are you looking for a date, a friend, a long-term relationship and/or marriage and children? You don't have to pick just one unless you want to be very clear that you are dating with the goal of marriage in mind, not just to have fun. But don't bother selecting friend; that's as noncommittal as possible and is a turnoff. Age range is a heavy question, and I'll address it later in its own section. Marital status asks if you would be willing to date someone who is single, divorced, or widowed. Would you date someone with kids and would you date someone who does or doesn't want kids? What level of Judaism do you prefer, and what level of education do you prefer? Would you date a smoker, and do you care if the person drinks often? Spend some time with this section and answer the questions that feel important to you. Leaving too many questions blank is suspicious, like you're willing to date just about anyone. And don't pick too many options for any one question either because, again, it looks like you're willing to date anyone who crosses your path. Don't be overly specific because no one will have every single characteristic in a profile that's too narrow, and then they won't contact you because they will think you wouldn't go for them since they don't fulfill all your preferences.

JDate: Likes and Interests

This is the cluster of multiple-choice questions that can quickly get overwhelming. You definitely want to answer these because if you don't, it looks like you didn't finish filling out your profile. Contrarily, you don't want to answer every single question because that can seem disingenuous as well. These questions mostly have to do with your hobbies, although there is an important one hiding in there: "My personality is best described as . . ." Take time choosing your answer to that one, and otherwise just answer as you see fit. Do not say that you snowboard under "My favorite physical activities" if you only hit the slopes once a season, and don't say you enjoy amusement parks "In my free time" when you only go once a year on your niece's birthday.

JDATE'S MOBILE APP: JPIX

JDate's new mobile platform is called JPix, and it is leaps-and-bounds better than the former mobile app. Now you can easily access JDate on-the-go—no more having to be in front of your computer. This is great! Since we all have smartphones glued to our hands, now there's really no excuse for not being active on JDate. Plus the app is free for Apple and Android devices.

JDATE: EXTRAS

JDate has added "Kibitz" and "The Color Code Compatibility" tabs to JDaters' profiles, but completing these sections is not a necessity. Kibitz asks a range of questions, but it won't permit you to view other people's answers to these questions unless you answer them on your profile as well. They are silly questions, and if you're bored you may answer a few, but if you answer all of them then you end up looking overly desperate. Color Code Compatibility is a personality traits test that tries to tell you if you're compatible with someone based on the color they've been designated by responding to a set of questions. Don't base your decision to contact someone or not on this test.

Perfect Match is a badge, or a graphic, located near the prospect's profile that gives you a numerical value in percentage form (i.e., 87%) of things you have in common. Even JDate states not to be discouraged if that number is low, but of course to be encouraged to reach out and make contact when it is on the higher end.

JDate: Likes, Flirts, Secret Admirer, Hot Lists, and Views

These five features allow JDaters to interact with each other's profiles. As you're reading through a profile, you have the option to "Like" every written answer, similar to how you can "Like" a Facebook post. This is a great way to let someone know that you have read their profile rather than just scanned their photos and sent them an email because they were a "match" for you. There is also a place to comment on written responses, but unless you have something very pertinent to say then don't say anything. For example, if under The Coolest Places I've Visited a person has written some obscure place that you've also visited, then you should say so, but, otherwise, leave it be.

Flirts are a great way to let someone know you are interested and to gauge that someone's interest in return. Click on the Flirt button under the profile name and biographical information. A Flirt is noncommittal, although the person sees who you are and can then click on your profile. If a person sends you a Flirt in return, then you can safely assume the attraction and interest is mutual and you can then send an email (I cover emails more in a section below). The only problem with a Flirt is that it forces you to send one of JDate's cheesy automated messages. The options are silly, but if your Flirt is followed up with an email where you make fun of the automated Flirt message you sent, then it can be cute.

Secret Admirer allows you to notify someone that you're interested in him or her, but it keeps your identity a secret at first. JDate gives you the option to click "Y," "M," or "N" for yes, maybe, or no for the Secret Admirer option on any prospect's profile. So let's say you're reading a profile, and you decide to click "Y" to become this prospect's Secret Admirer. If the prospect has already viewed your profile or will eventually view your profile and he or she also clicked "Y" to become your Secret Admirer, you will be informed by JDate that there is a match. If the prospect clicks the "N" or "M," then he or she will never know who you were. This is a great feature because no one gets hurt.

You can add prospects to your Favorites list by clicking on the star icon below a profile to easily track that person's online activity. Remember: If you Favorite someone, he or she can see that you did so on Hot Lists. (Unless you change your profile settings.)

Views allows you to see who is checking out your profile, so remember that others can see if you've viewed theirs. There are ways to prevent others from seeing when and how often you're viewing their profile by hiding your own profile, but that means no one else can see you either. And that doesn't make any sense, does it? You're on the website because you're single and want to meet people, so allow those people to see you and know you viewed them. One of the first things people click when they log on to JDate is the "who viewed me" option—they'll see who checked them out and then view them back. When someone with whom you share a mutual interest makes a repeat viewing it is a secret thrill, just as if you were at a bar and saw someone you were interested in continuously make eye contact.

JDATE: AGE RANGE

How do you pick the right age range? Most people do not do this correctly, though it's a simple way to both narrow down your number of prospects and get you more matches at the same time. In general, you should be looking in at least a ten-year range. One exception is if you yourself are on the younger side and at the bottom of the age spectrum (between twenty-one and twenty-five years old), in which case your age range can only be a few years on each side of your own age. Sometimes the age range will be more than ten years, and sometimes the bulk of it will be below your age while at other times it will be pretty evenly balanced on either side of your age.

This is not an exact science. If there are far too many prospects showing up as matches using this guide, then try to narrow down other preferences that you may have been too broad with before fiddling with the numbers. Did you include "associate's degree" as the level of the prospect's education when you really prefer someone with a minimum of a "bachelor's degree"? Then eliminate it. Anywhere where you may have extended your boundaries with the sincere intention of wanting to see who was out there can be narrowed down slightly. If there is nowhere to trim and you are still overwhelmed by the number of prospects who fall within

Age	Minimum Range	Maximum Range	Notes
25	21	32	A good range for this age in its entirety although it's more than 10 years
30	24	38	Try to narrow this down on each side to get closer to a 10-year spread
35	27	43	Would you connect with someone eight years older or younger?
40	33	50	How mature of a 40-year-old are you?
45	37	53	How mature of a 45-year-old are you?
50	40	60	Do you prefer someone older or younger?
55	45	65	A 45-year-old may not be in the same place as you, the same goes for a 65-year-old
60	50	70	The older you get, the wider the spectrum can be as your priorities shift
65	55	75	Trim the spectrum as you see fit
70	60	80	If you don't have enough options, widen your age range

your preferences, then skim one year off the age range at a time, alternating between minimum and maximum. Conversely, if there's only one or two pages of prospects at any given time, then you are probably setting too strict a standard. Will you only accept someone exactly your age who is a Conservative Jew with a postdoctoral degree of some kind who keeps kosher? Something has got to give.

JDATE: EMAILS

Eventually you will have a nice assortment of prospects who fit the bulk of your preferences and with whom you've exchanged Flirts, been matched as Secret Admirers, and selected as a Favorite (or perhaps none of the above, but you have both viewed each other and both see a connection). Then it's time to begin the exchange of emails. Though women tend to appreciate men making the initial contact, remember that this is only an email, and it's perfectly okay if a woman writes first. If you've both made it clear that you're interested via JDate's tools, then there's no reason why either of you shouldn't make the move of sending the first email. So ladies, don't be shy!

When you write your message make sure it is not about you! A prospect can read enough about you by reading your profile. The message should be about why you like the other person, what caught your eye, and what you have in common. Make the message specific to the person you're writing to, and add a compliment or two for good measure. End with a question about something you have in common. The email should be more than three sentences but not more than a long paragraph. And by no means should you ever copy and paste a generic email; it's always obvious!

If you're on the receiving end of an email, you can easily check to make sure the writer read your profile by looking for specifics. If you think the writer is attractive and you like their profile and their message, then go ahead and write back. But don't wait too long. You should reply within the next day or two, just as you would if the message were a voice mail to return. The reply should consist of a thank you, a return compliment, the answer to the question, and a question of your own.

In response to a reply, you might include your answers to any questions plus a few more conversational tidbits—give a bit of new information that's not too personal mixed with more questions about the other person—and then finally end the email with the request for a phone number (or, the offering of a phone number).

If you receive a reply to your reply, then your response should be the final email exchange, with each of you having written two emails. Your message could consist of a bit of conversation plus your phone number, but don't ask any more questions as you don't want to give the person a reason to email you rather than call.

The key to Internet dating is to get off the Internet as soon as possible. Think about it: Because of the profile questions, you already know more about the other person than you would after the first date. So if you start trading long and intense letters, then all you're going to do is create unneeded anticipation. A lot of people can have good rapport on paper, but you don't want to build up expectations you can't meet. You'll have plenty of time to email, instant message, and text once you're dating.

If you've received a phone number, pick up the phone within forty-eight hours. Don't call during the day when most people are at work, and don't call on the weekends when most people have plans. Make the first phone call on a weekday evening. If you're going to dial, then you want the other person to pick up, so call when you think they're most likely going to answer.

Once you get on the phone, cut to the chase. Again, you don't want spend too much time chatting before you know if there's chemistry in person. Make plans for drinks sometime within the next week, leaving the evening open in case drinks lead to dinner. First-date tips can be found in Chapter 8.

INTERNET REALITY

If people at a party or bar could have the basics from JDate's profile page pop-up in a thought bubble over their heads, that would be very helpful indeed. Imagine if you saw someone who piqued your interest and suddenly his or her religion, status, age, denomination, education, relationship history, and career was listed on his or her side like a nutrition label. Not too much information would have to be divulged— just enough to let you know if the person meets even a few of your criteria. Not Jewish? Okay, move on. Not single? Next! Under twenty-five? Um, keep it moving. And so on.

Then, all you would need to incorporate is the "Secret Admirer" feature and you would be set. That feature is by far my favorite; it would spare a lot of feelings if there were some way to utilize it in noncyberspace situations. Think about it: All you'd have to do is send some kind of mental signal upon checking out the other person, giving him or her a "yes," "no," or "maybe." Once the other person sends their signal in return, then you two are free to either meet or move on. Eliminating the risk of rejection by knowing the interest is mutual would probably help to create thousands of couples that would otherwise not have met. Most people are single simply because they're afraid to stick their necks out.

True, it might take away some of the mystery and the fun of the chase, but it also paves the way for people who stand in the shadows or blend into the background. But just because two people are Secret Admirers doesn't mean they will automatically like each other and get married and live happily ever after. Oh no, there's still plenty of work to be done, but at least this way you could increase your odds of meeting someone.

So how do you make the Secret Admirer feature a part of your noncyber life? It's all about sending signals and being obvious about it. Forget about subtlety—it's not all it's cracked up to be. No more glancing over and looking away and glancing over and looking away and hoping that's enough. Both parties must, must, must make eye contact and smile for a minimum of three seconds—five is even better. Count down in your head if you have to, but don't look away too soon! Make eye contact, hold it, and smile. Turn your body toward your prospect to show you're open and approachable; don't cross your arms across your chest or put them on your hips, and make sure you smile not only with your mouth but with your eyes, too. If you have friends around you, try to isolate yourself (a slow trip to the bathroom or a walk outside for some fresh air) so the intimidation factor is eliminated.

Once you start talking, show your interest by maintaining eye contact and not looking over the other person's shoulder to see who else is out there. Listen intently to what the other person is saying and either exchange a related story of your own experience or ask a follow-up question. Make sure you do a little of each so you are both learning about the other person and allowing them to learn about you as well. No one wants to feel like they are in a therapy session because they're being asked too many questions, nor does anyone want to walk away realizing they don't know a thing about you. And once again, a little bit of good manners goes a long way. If you decide after a few minutes of conversation that you no longer are a match, then simply and politely say, "It was nice to meet you," and excuse yourself to go see if you hit it off with someone else.

THE DOWN SIDE

Not everything about Internet dating is positive. It doesn't seem like a big stretch to connect the advent of technology directly to the recent statistics that show an overall, across-the-board, delayed age of marriage—although it might not be the only reason, nor the most important reason, the connection is probable. Email, text messages, and even helpful tools like JDate have only added to the confusion and complexities of dating. Suddenly we have more ways to meet potentials and just as many ways to screw things up. Courtship seems to have been replaced by the Wi-Fi signal. Technology has lead to lethargy.

Long gone are the days of replaying and deciphering a message on your answering machine until the tape wears thin; instead, you get to decipher a one-line email. Long gone are the days of showing up on time for a date because you would never think of letting the person sit there unaware; instead, you receive a text with a sad excuse. Long gone are the days of meeting someone Jewish at a singles mixer held at your local temple; instead, JDate will advise you of your online matches with a prescheduled email alert. Long gone are the days of scribbling your name and number on a napkin; instead, you just tell the guy or gal to add you on Facebook. Long gone are the days of calling ten times a day until you catch your crush at home; instead, caller ID means you phone once and hang up before the machine comes on because you know the person will see your number recorded on the handset and will hopefully take the hint to call you back.

Do you miss the more organic "butterflies in the stomach" feeling that came with wondering when someone was going to call versus being able to chart their every move via Facebook, Twitter, and even JDate? The mystery and intrigue is palpably missing from this technologically advanced generation's romantic overtures. How can singles stay proactive on the market without getting tangled up in all the wires? Keep it simple and don't let technology get the best of you. Sign up for JDate, but, once you make a connection, get offline immediately. Don't text someone until you've been on a few dates, and then only once a day (at the most!) during work. Try to control yourself from adding your new flame on Facebook, instant messaging, or even emailing until you're in a bona fide relationship. Save the conversation to be had in person, face-to-face.

You can even use this topic as a conversation piece: the embarrassing photo you accidentally emailed to your boss; the ridiculously high number of friend requests you have yet to accept on Facebook; and the absurd way you were once dumped via text message. Then parlay the conversation into how you want to handle a new relationship with (or without) these newer forms of communication.

CAUTION!

On top of everything else, singles have to now be careful they don't get scammed via online dating. Some of the scams are emotional, some are financial, but falling prey to a catfish stings no matter how you got yourself into the situation (there's a reason why catfish aren't kosher!). There are the prospects who seem perfect online but who in person are not exactly what they said they were. That's a normal pothole of online dating, when people can hide their crazy behind a computer screen. But there are other types of lies you need to be aware of when opening yourself up online.

Even on JDate and other Jewish Internet dating sites, singles might want to confirm that a prospect is actually Jewish. Non-Jews are joining JDate and other sites because they know (probably better than we Chosen Ones know) that Jews make great spouses and parents. Some sites give you the option to view Only Jews, but none of them authenticate a person's heritage. Why someone would go on a Jewish dating site and lie about their religion is beyond me, but it happens. I believe they should at the very least be honest and upfront about it and give people the option to choose. My take: If they're lying about being Jewish on a Jewish dating site, then chances are they're there scamming for a hookup, which brings me to the next type of shadesters singles need to look out for online.

There are people, called catfish, who spend the time and money to create an online profile just to find dates that will end with a one-night stand. They'll tell you what you want to hear, romance you, and probably use liquor to relax you and lower your inhibitions. Remember that with your online profile you have answered many personal questions, which these players use like ammunition with which they can ploy you into their good graces. If it's too good to be true, then it probably is. Don't get sucked into their scheme. There is not one person on this planet who will agree with you about everything and think that the sun, moon, and stars should revolve around you. If that's what you're hearing, then try to listen to your subconscience telling you that something isn't kosher. Most Internet daters will probably get conned by a player at least once. It's that perfect prospect who never called you again. Don't take it personally—it happens—but just don't make the same mistake twice.

And then there are the scam artists, the people who are looking for desperate and vulnerable singles. It may sound obvious, but never, ever send money to someone you've only met online. If someone claims to be from out of the country and says he or she is moving here and then suddenly needs some extra cash to visit you, don't believe it's your beshert who happens to live thousands of miles and $1300 away. It's not. Your bank account will thank you later. Don't give up too much personal information on your account either, as you can set yourself up for identity theft—as stated before, don't use your last name and never offer your social security number or full birthdate or credit card information. Even one of those pieces of information is enough for a professional criminal to use to steal your identity. If you've only met online, then you really don't know who the other person is on the other side—it could be anybody, remember that—which is why I strongly recommended meeting right away. If someone doesn't want to meet, there's a reason. Heed my warning and move on. Don't give him or her a second thought because I can guarantee they are not who they say they are in some way, shape, or form.

Trust your instincts online and have realistic expectations. People are going to stretch the truth and build themselves up a little bigger (or skinnier or taller) and better, and that's expected, but, if someone seems a little too perfect, don't hesitate to guard your heart and wallet. Still, JDate and other Jewish dating websites are well worth the risk as long as you have your guard up. Once someone passes muster then let your guard down, no different than you would if you met someone out and about!

 ## Julie

A few years ago when Julie was in her midtwenties, she threw her hands up in despair and asked me to help her find a nice, Jewish guy. I mentioned JDate, and a guttural sound emanated from her throat while her face distorted into a look of disgust, the corners of her lips turning down while her upper lip peaked into a snarl, her eyes becoming slits and her jaw tensing. When she finally recovered from her bout with repulsion, she said, simply, *"Ew."*

I couldn't help but start laughing, and then I shared my story with her: I remember being in my early twenties and thinking how absurd it sounded to have to resort to Internet dating to find a boyfriend. Back then, I also thought I was too good for JDate, but once I hit the ripe old age of twenty-five, I succumbed to the pressure. I signed up for a JDate membership (with my mom's credit card, of course) and ate humble pie. After years of thumbing my nose at the idea, I found dozens upon dozens of totally eligible bachelors—some that I already knew, and some I didn't—and I was happily surprised to know I was in good (and good-looking) company. I found myself enjoying scanning the thousands of Jewish men displayed on my computer screen.

I told Julie that I, too, had preconceived notions about JDate and was surprised to find good-looking guys on there, and that I wondered why these guys would have to resort to Internet dating. But then I realized I was on there, too, so why shouldn't they be? JDate is not just for losers, not just for rejects, not just for socially awkward dorks who don't know how to say "hello" without stammering. I told her JDate is a place where all Jews go to look for their beshert. Everyone is on there: Jews who don't even go to Jewish events, Jews who may not even identify as Jewish otherwise, and, even, sometimes, non-Jews!

I explained to Julie her odds of finding dates on JDate would be even better than the year she studied abroad in

Israel since these guys are on there to meet their future wives. She could vet the prospects by narrowing down her criteria at her behest, whether by area, age, or however her currently critical heart desires.

As the JDate conversation continued at a dinner party, most of the people, guys and gals alike, all proudly stated they, too, were on JDate. Julie quickly became the odd woman out, and I think she even became excited at the idea of signing up. She discovered JDate is not the place where desperate people go but rather it's okay, and even cool, to say you're on JDate.

Natalie

Natalie and I have been corresponding on and off over the past few years since her divorce, and as she has flitted in and out of flings. She's been on and off JDate using the free membership and is finally ready to take the leap and pay for a few months, but she wanted an Extreme Profile Makeover first. I was stunned after she gave me her profile name because her answers to the In My Words section were not a reflection of the Natalie I had come to know. She is a woman full of energy and enthusiasm and gobs of personality, but her profile made her seem quiet and reserved. I needed to help Natalie figure out how to let her personality come across in a way that would attract the same amount of men as she does in person (only minus the jerks). Since I wasn't going to be the one writing the emails, I needed Natalie to write her In My Words answers on her own as well.

I implored her to start her rewrite with high energy and to keep it up throughout the profile. If it took her weeks, then so be it. And if she needed to send me one answer at a time to tweak (tracking my changes so she could see where I was injecting her personality into the essays), then I was willing to do that, too. In the end, Natalie and I only had to work on her profile for a few weeks before it was up to snuff because once she saw how I edited her responses she was able to pick up on how to allow her personality to come through on paper, or rather, screen.

Mike

As I've explained before, Mike disses JDate in public but secretly has a hidden profile. He doesn't contact anyone, but he peruses to see if there are any women out there who fit his ridiculously strict requirements. If he does meet someone at a mixer, he uses JDate as a sort of background check. Mike is thirty-three, and he has chosen a narrow age range for his prospective matches, from twenty-eight to thirty-two. He wants a woman taller than five foot six, lighter than 130 pounds (or who identifies as a "slim" body type), only a Reform or Traditional Jew, with at least a bachelor's degree and what he considers a "real" job, even though that seems to be subjective from prospect to prospect according to what kind of mood he's in or how attractive he finds a particular woman. He wants an unmarried woman with no kids who has selected no more than a "long-term relationship" and who doesn't smoke but drinks socially. *Whew!* Oh, and let's not forget the need for the woman to be overtly romantic and affectionate. Needless to say, Mike will most likely be single for a very long time if he continues with this mind-set.

 ## Lauren

JDate was just getting going when Lauren met her now-ex-husband nearly fifteen years ago, so she didn't think she would ever need it when she heard her single girlfriends discussing it. Now it's a reality for her, and she is warming up to the idea little by little. She has looked through the site as a visitor and has had some friends lend her their log-ins so she can see who is out there. She likes what she sees so far and is tinkering with what she will say in her answers and which pictures she will use. I gave her a few nuggets of advice specifically for divorcées and those with kids: State you're divorced in your status, it's a fact and you can't deny it. DO NOT go into detail about the divorce in your profile; simply say you are looking forward to finding the person who suits you now, you have no regrets since you have spectacular children, and you are excited to meet the person you hope to enjoy the prime of your life with. Aside from that, answer the questions for yourself and not in regard to being someone's ex-wife or someone's mother. Yes, Lauren is looking for someone who will make a great step-dad—and someone who possibly already is a great dad—but she also needs to find someone who is better suited for the woman she is now at forty-one years old and not the young lady she was at twenty-six when she met her now-ex-husband. Lauren's age range should start at thirty-eight and stretch to forty-nine. She should be willing to date someone who is single or divorced, someone with or without kids. Of course, she will probably have a deeper connection to a divorcé with children, but that doesn't mean a single guy couldn't fill the role.

 ## Beth

Beth's JDate journey has been an ever-changing one, as she has been on and off JDate in between relationships since JDate launched in 1997. Her profile changed drastically when she came out of the closet, and, on top of that, her profile had to be adjusted along with her age. Her preferences now at forty-eight are vastly different than they were when she was thirty-two. She has accepted the fact she won't have children, so she's not looking for someone with maternal instincts, although she would be open to a single mother, a divorcée, and even a widow. She is also open to women as young as thirty-eight as well as women who are in their mid- to late-fifties. Although Beth has established herself in Chicago, she is now willing to relocate. Her preferences were narrow in her thirties and she is now regretting not listening to people who told her she would never find a woman (or, previously, a man) who could fit into the mold she expected. Beth's biggest challenge now is to not let her disillusionment about dating in the past effect her future dating, as she automatically expects disappointment. She is trying to accept what comes to her and see the silver lining, but she isn't always successful at it.

 ## David

Everyone in David's social circle keeps telling David to go on JDate, but he's not quite ready yet. He's attracting enough women on his own and through setups, plus he knows that JDate is kind of a meat market for men in their early sixties (and if he wasn't so humble, he would also admit it's because he looks so good for his age!).

What he doesn't know is that his daughters have created a profile for him. This type of profile can work well, as it's endearing to have your kids posting on your behalf (conversely, it's not cute to have your parents posting for you), but eventually his kids will have to come clean because no setup will go smoothly if the date is hiding a secret about how David's daughters know her. The girls know what their father likes and needs: a woman between fifty and sixty-five who looks young and has an active lifestyle; a woman who will take care of their father and be a caring step-mom and an awesome grandmother to their future kids.

They prefer someone who has been through something similar to their father, as losing the love of his life was tough enough and would continue to be tough if he was partnered with someone who couldn't empathize. But they also don't want their father in a relationship with someone with whom he will constantly be commiserating about their respective tragedies. Losing their mother was devastating, but they want their father to find happiness for what will hopefully be another thirty-plus years. Their profile gets so many responses they have been able to narrow down their preferences further than they thought they would ever need to, and they still are digging through the profiles to find the ones with the right amount of pep and personality.

Chapter 6

✳ MODES OF COMMUNICATION ▶

DATING IS NOTHING IF NOT confusing. I get tons of emails asking for help with conundrums such as, "He calls me regularly but doesn't ask me out," or, "He texted me after our date but I haven't heard from him since." A majority of the blame belongs to the current popular forms of communication: email, instant messages, and texts. Not knowing the tone, the sarcasm, or the intent of a written message can be a cause for confusion.

PHONE CALLS

In this day and age, it's hard not to make a phone call. I accidentally call people all the time when I forget to lock the keypad on my cell phone. Still, I get more emails from women asking why men don't call than emails with any other type of question or complaint. They want to know why guys ask for their phone numbers at a singles mixer and then never call. This is a question that's been asked since the invention of the telephone, and there will probably never be a satisfactory answer. Herein lies the confusion: If you're a single man and are at happy hour or a networking event, then a woman can rightly assume you're there to meet someone just like she is. You went to all the effort to approach her, get to know her, and ask her for her phone number. So why no phone call? Women also have been known to make the effort to get a phone number and then never bother calling. No one is innocent when it comes to a handheld device.

Was your conquest complete after getting the digits? Did you suddenly suffer a case of amnesia? Is it possible you dropped your phone into a cup of water while hugging someone and lost all your numbers? (This is an actual excuse I was once told.) Or could it be that your ex-girlfriend was at the event, got jealous seeing you talking to an attractive woman, realized she still had feelings for you, and now you're back together? (Again, this happened to me.) But who really knows? Women are left to ponder the possibilities for eternity.

Another scenario women ask me about is a common and hurtful one: Women think they've been on a really great first date, they shared a nice kiss at the end of the night, they were told they would be getting a call soon, and then . . . nothing. Really? Come on guys, call if you say you're going to call, and otherwise, don't say you're going to call. It's simple.

By the way, women can be just as bad about not returning phone calls. Sometimes a woman will give a man her phone number just to get the guy to go away. So when the phone rings and she doesn't recognize the number on the caller ID, she will let it go to voice mail and then never return the call. This is not nice, and it's just as bad as not making the phone call to begin with.

TEXT MESSAGES

One excuse I often hear from men is they'd rather text than call to save time. If you really wanted to see a woman, then you would take the time and make the effort to place a phone call. It doesn't have to be a long one. You can even start off the conversation by saying you're busy but want to make plans to get together. Still, some men would rather text "what r u up 2?" Seriously? You're going to ask a woman out via text message? A text does not take the place of a phone call. Period.

Texting has become the bane of my existence as a dating expert. I understand its convenience, I get how it can be a subtle form of communication, and now that it's part of our everyday lives, I can't imagine not having the option to use it. But when it comes to dating, we need to revert to the prehistoric era of phone calls and answering machines. If you want to send someone a signal that you're interested, then simply pick up the phone and call. Texting, "hey, wazzup," is not going to clearly portray the message you intended. The problem is, I think this is what texters are hedging their bets on—if they find out the prospect is not interested, they can claim it was just a friendly text, whereas a phone call's intention is more obvious.

The amount of miscommunication, confusion, and discord that can come from 160 characters on a two-and-a-half-square-inch screen sent via the Short Message Service (SMS) gateway is infinitesimal. To top it off, the amount of time it takes to type the message, abbreviating certain words and phrases to use fewer characters and keep it to one text and still be smooth and charming, is dumbfounding. You could have had a full-length phone conversation in that time and accomplished a lot more if you simply had the guts to dial a phone number instead of an acronym. And if you both have an iPhone or use What's App or some other free texting service then it can get even more out of hand with not having any limitations with texting. The simple fact is that men and women both will always, always, always prefer a phone call. If he or she doesn't answer, leave a message. If you don't receive a call back, don't waste your time by following up with a text—just cut your losses and move on.

If you like someone, it doesn't matter how busy you are at work, how sick your grandmother is, or where you're traveling. You can make up any excuse in the book, but the simple fact is, if you were interested, you would call and, if the other person were interested, he or she would call back. Once you can grasp that concept, dating will get a whole lot easier. It will continue to be disappointing at times, but it will get easier.

A HOW-TO TUTORIAL

This is how to use our many modes of communication in an effective and productive way:

1. Select the dial screen from the phone app on your home screen.
2. Dial the number of the hottie you met less than forty-eight hours ago.
3. Say hello and begin a conversation.

I'm kidding—kind of. It really is that easy, but that can be putting the cart before the horse. You meet someone, whether online or in person, and eventually exchange phone numbers. Yes, in the old days a man was expected to call a woman first, and, though that may still be how things happen in any given relationship, each pair and every situation is unique. If a guy says he is going to call you, then let him call you. Men like the chance to be on one end of a phone call with a woman who is happy to hear from him. But if a gal says she will call or if no one made any specific arrangements, then there's no reason a woman can't call first, and she, too, can enjoy calling someone who is happy to hear from her.

The first phone call needs to happen within a day or two of meeting. Use the following schedule as a guideline:

Received phone number:	Make phone call on:
Sunday	Monday by 9:00 PM or Tuesday by 9:00 PM
Monday	Tuesday by 9:00 PM or Wednesday by 9:00 PM
Tuesday	Wednesday by 9:00 PM or Thursday by 9:00 PM
Wednesday	Thursday by 9:00 PM or Friday by 12:00 PM
Thursday	Friday by 12:00 PM or Saturday between 10:00 AM and 2:00 PM
Friday	Saturday between 10:00 AM and 2:00 PM or Sunday by 9:00 PM
Saturday	Sunday by 9:00 PM or Monday by 9:00 PM

First phone calls have a deadline. If you don't put the effort in to call within two days, then why should the other person make the effort to answer with excitement? The first phone call has a time limit, too—around ten minutes. Use the time to exchange pleasantries; discuss how great or ironic or fun or dramatic it was to meet. Then make plans using this schedule as a guideline:

Day of first call:	Day for first date:
Sunday	Tuesday evening or Wednesday evening
Monday	Wednesday evening Thursday evening
Tuesday	Thursday evening or Friday night
Wednesday	Friday night or Saturday night (or you can wait until Sunday afternoon if you're not ready for Prime Time Date Night)
Thursday	Saturday night or Sunday afternoon
Friday	Sunday afternoon or Monday evening
Saturday	Monday evening or Tuesday evening

This is where it can get complicated. Sometimes you meet someone whom you want to see right away, which is why you should plan a date within two to three days of the phone call. Other times, you want to wait until the weekend, Prime Time Date Night, to make a date really special. Waiting until the weekend is a big move and lets the other person know you think they're worth Prime Time Date

Night right off the bat, because not everyone is. But sometimes you can have the best of both worlds because, if a midweek date goes really well, then you can have a second date that weekend, making for two dates within the same week and creating some great momentum.

A phone call should be made within a day or two after a great date, too, but, again, it can be kept to a maximum of about ten minutes. This is the phone call where you tell the other person how great of a time you had on the date and you make plans for another date. The first few phone calls are not for spending hours on the phone getting to know each other; leave those conversations for the dates. Rather, the first few phone calls are for making plans and showing consistency—calling when you say you're going to call and being flexible about making plans. Once you've established that you are "dating" (which means you've gone on numerous dates, not just one or two), then you can start having those marathon phone calls that leave your phone battery running on empty and you exhausted the next day at work. This is also the point where you can begin sending texts, but for casual purposes only—do not engage in serious topics or be overly flirtatious via SMS.

If a first or second date doesn't go well or there wasn't any chemistry, then you really ought to make some kind of contact to let the other person know there won't be another date. This is the place where text messaging is acceptable. You can simply send a text and say, "Thank you for a nice date. I wish you the best of luck in finding someone." Odds are the other person already knows there wasn't a connection and won't be surprised by the text. If you've been on more than two dates, then this text is not appropriate. You can find more on this topic in Chapter 9, Poly-Dating.

♥ Julie

After weeks of emailing and texting, Julie was finally ready to meet Brian, a good-looking Jewish lawyer who recently moved to town. Unfortunately, the effort they put in to meet each other was not quite enough.

Brian contacted Julie on JDate, and after exchanging a few emails he asked her, via JDate email, to meet him for a glass of wine. She responded with her phone number. His response: his phone number. Julie was confused about what her next step should be. After a few more emails, Brian again asked her to meet him, this time for gelato over the weekend. She again responded with her phone number and suggested they make plans by phone. His response: a text saying hi and asking how she was doing. The nonexistent relationship went from confusing to frustrating.

Julie wrote an email telling Brian she wasn't a text person, and he told her he wasn't a phone person. It was enough to make a girl give up, and Julie was just about to throw in the towel. I advised her to stop playing his game and to not respond to his texts. It worked. He finally called the next day to ask her out, but, by that point, Julie was already over it.

♥ Natalie

Natalie is guilty of not returning phone calls. Recently, she met a guy and they exchanged phone numbers. After spending a few hours talking on the phone (her first mistake), they made plans for a date. Once she was on the date, she realized the chemistry just wasn't there, but she was still willing to give him another chance and accepted his invitation for making plans for a second date (her second mistake). But she never returned his subsequent calls. About two weeks later, for no other reason than to clear her conscience, she called him. She called during a time when she didn't think he was going to answer and luckily for her, his voice mail cued up. So she simply left a message apologizing for not returning his phone calls and wished him well.

Natalie's move was good for karma because she, like every other single, hates it when calls go unanswered, especially when a prospect has appeared to be interested. Hopefully, she learned her lesson and will listen to her instincts while on a date so she doesn't give off misleading signs, which can lead to unwelcome phone calls.

 ## Mike

Mike meets girls often and easily but drops the ball soon after. The one consistent thread? He communicates solely by text: He texts to test the waters, check the calendar, and finalize plans, and he even sends postdate wrap-up messages. Mike has dinner with friends and spends the entire time checking his phone and furiously tapping the screen, his eyes lighting up every time the screen glows with a new message and the table shaking every time the phone vibrates.

Mike's excuse for texting the woman he is currently in a texting tug-of-war with is that, when he does call, she doesn't answer and texts him instead. It's clear to me the woman is playing games with Mike, but he is intrigued by this rather than turned off. I repeatedly give Mike advice to call her, but he makes up excuses left and right even as he becomes more and more frustrated by her confusing texts. My bottom line remains that he should avoid any further miscommunication by refraining from texting her and by simply calling her. Mike continues to wonder how to translate her game-playing messages and what kind of subtext he can formulate in his reply. *Ugh!* I keep trying to impress upon him why a phone call would be the most telling and would save him time and energy.

No matter what I say or how much I insist, he is relentless in his support of texting. Is he afraid of rejection or does he lack confidence in his speech? Maybe he simply isn't that interested or intrigued enough by this woman to make the effort to call, or maybe he doesn't really want the relationship to come to fruition. Each of these possibilities is realistic. But they're the same anxieties singles have had for eternity, and resorting to text messages is not the solution.

 Lauren

Lauren was set up with a friend of a friend who liked to text her, and, as a single mom, she is privy to texting since she is usually sitting on the sidelines of a soccer game or in the bleachers of some rehearsal or practice. But texting her girlfriends to vent or make plans is not the same as flirting. Lauren hasn't flirted this way in so long that she is rusty at deciphering wit and sarcasm, and she ran into quite the conundrum with this new beau when she couldn't figure out if he was being serious or not. She ended up having to call him to ask and was super embarrassed to find out he

HOW TO WOO A JEW

was just trying to be cute. Lauren vowed then and there to leave her texting behind when it came to dating. It was difficult enough for her to start putting herself out there, and she didn't want to have to also deal with the stress of translating abbreviations.

Lauren has been asked out on quite a few dates, but with her custody schedule she can't always make plans right away. A few times she ended up spending hours on the phone with a guy after her kids were asleep, and then, when she finally met him, she was really pissed at herself for wasting some quality, and much needed, sleep on this guy before they had even met. Lauren never thought to ask her single girlfriends how to text and talk before dating; she never realized it was going to be an issue. Luckily she didn't get hurt, and she has learned her lessons.

 ## Beth

One of Beth's biggest pet peeves is when a woman says she's going to call and then doesn't, regardless whether they have just met or have found each other on JDate or have already gone on a date or two. Getting rejected without any closure is something Beth has a hard time accepting. She understands if a woman isn't interested. But when the woman doesn't come clean about her feelings, this infuriates Beth. Beth is ashamed, but she actually has sent nasty emails, left dirty voice mails, and texted words not fit for print to these women who she considers cowards and losers. I pointed out to her that at least she found out this way before spending too much time on these women and not after a few months of dating. Beth does have a point though—either don't say you're going to call, or send some kind of message that you're no longer interested so the other person can move on. And Beth should lay off the ugly follow-ups as they only make her look ugly.

 ## David

David is not technologically challenged, but he also doesn't use texting for anything but to let his family and friends know if he's running late. David also isn't a huge phone-talker, but he understands it is a means to an end. What David is is a gentleman, which means he does call when he says he's going to and if he's not interested he calls to say so. David is the perfect communicator, but it has gotten him in a little bit of trouble. He calls to respectfully and gently let women know there isn't a match and ends up on the phone with women crying and trying to convince him otherwise and begging for another chance. David holds his ground, but he wants to figure out a way to still give the women closure without getting stuck having to reject them twice in one phone conversation, especially since he's only trying to do the right thing.

iCRUSH

BETWEEN JDATE, FACEBOOK, Instagram, and other online networking sites, it's easy to track the life of someone you're interested in. It's also easy to cross the line between snooping and stalking. There are ways to check in on a crush without getting caught, and there are ways to stop someone from checking in on you. Don't feel ashamed to confess your cyber-stalking addiction; it's unfortunately a reality, and a lot of people are doing it even if no one is admitting it.

Cyber stalking usually starts as a thoughtless glance to see if a JDate crush has read your email. All it takes is a foray into your JDate inbox and a quick click on "sent messages," and you can easily see if an email has been opened. Cyber stalking has the chance to get amped up if your email hasn't been read and you're wondering if you should take it personally. Clicking on your crush's profile to see if he or she has logged on since you sent the email seems innocent enough, but, if you're logging on to JDate multiple times throughout the day while you're at work, you're harboring an unhealthy obsession. That crush can see when you've logged in and when you've checked his or her profile.

Although I recommend only checking JDate once or twice a day, there are precautions you can take to make sure you at least don't get caught if you're totally obsessed (because "obsessed" is exactly what you are!). You can change your profile to "hidden" when you want to check in on your crushes without them knowing you're viewing them. But every once in a while, unhide your profile and view your crushes so they know you're still interested.

If you find yourself Googling your crush before you've even met, you need to take your hand off the mouse and slowly step away from the computer. Once you start dating, it's perfectly reasonable to want to do a background check, but, when you go on a JDate knowing more information than what was supplied on the profile, then your gig is up. Unless of course there is something suspicious going on. If someone seems too good to be true, then he or she probably is, so use Google sparingly in that case. Put the person's name in quotes, and the World Wide Web can confirm your love interest really graduated from Princeton—just look for his or her name listed on the Alumni Association page. See if the prospect and his or her alleged career appear on LinkedIn. You can also verify if your date really runs in marathons—look for the race websites, and the prospect's name will be recorded next to his or her time. (You should also Google yourself every once in a while to make sure the links that pop up really are about you.) As for any criminal activity, the name will pop up on local news channel websites and the local sheriff's department website, in which case you'll have to decide for yourself what to do next.

As soon as you confirm these few major details, then get off the computer and go on the date. If you can't find any information to give you confidence, then consider asking your date some detailed questions to subtly dig around and see if there are signs that point to this person being fake—and you can always just cancel the date if you're feeling too insecure.

The same goes for Facebook. Once you add a crush on Facebook, you're going to fixate on who you know in common, who that girl or guy is in the pictures, and what those inside jokes mean between your crush and his or her friends. The longer you wait to add your crush to Facebook, the better. Eventually it will be a nice avenue to use for a character check so you can find out who he or she is friends with, what groups he or she belongs to, and what events he or she is attending. You can also look at photos to see if she is scantily clad or if he is in photos featuring alcohol or drugs.

If you're cyber stalking once you're dating, you have to be careful. When you're telling each other stories, you have to remember which tidbits of information your date told you and which you found out online. When you're meeting a prospect's friends for the first time, remember you only saw their pictures online and haven't actually met them before. You should probably wait until you're in a serious relationship to fess up to your online forays. Chances are the other person is guilty of the same thing!

I would tell you to try and avoid cyber stalking if possible, but the reality is it has spread like a virus, and if you're not doing it then you're already a step behind in the dating world. But if you really like someone, it may be worth a shot to try and not use the Internet and instead take the prospect for his or her word.

You may go through many phases when you don't necessarily want to be on JDate but you want to keep tabs on the new singles signing up. Though I don't condone this, it's a fact that many people will let their memberships expire and then hide their profiles for some time and use JDate and Facebook to try and find the people they're interested in.

While you can do what I'm about to describe, it's not exactly ethical, and I'm all for keeping it above-board. As Leviticus says, "You shall not cheat your fellow," and this is definitely a cheat. It works like this: If you have an expired JDate membership, you can't contact people, but you can take some of their background information, use the search function on Facebook, and try to find them there. JDate is no dummy though. They have filters set up so you can't put any variations of an email address, instant messenger screen name, or what have you (and when they remove the random letters—.com or AIM or gmail—to circumvent your attempts you end up with typos that make you appear uneducated, so double check your profile after publishing it), but people will often use their same photos for their profiles on JDate and other social networking sites, since it's usually their best photos, so they are likely easy enough to find. You can use keywords such as the city she lives in, his age, the college she attended, and his job industry to search for a prospect on Facebook—these are all things JDate asks for when you set up a profile—narrow down your search using whatever information you have.

Once you find your crush on Facebook, you can check to see if you have any friends in common. Chances are you do. Contact those mutual friends and let them know that you saw someone on JDate who they happen to know and ask them to connect you. Or, simply reinstate your JDate account and reach out right there—no meddling friends needed.

If you want to participate in helping singletons reach you online but off JDate, then do what you can to facilitate the search. Use the same profile photo in both accounts, use your first name in your JDate profile, and make sure to offer the information in your JDate profile that would assist a search on Facebook and vice-versa. Leaving out pertinent information such as current city, hometown, high school, college, company name, and so forth will make it difficult for people who want to try and meet you.

Don't be frightened if you're the receiver of a Facebook email from a stranger who says they saw you on JDate. It's flattering. Do due diligence and follow-up by checking out their profile on JDate to see if he or she is someone you have viewed or would be willing to give a chance to. And respond even if you are not interested. No harm, no foul, right? So why not send back a quick note saying thanks for the interest but you don't think it's a match. But if you are interested, then you will have a cute story to share about how you met your beshert!

Interweb dating is just one more tool to utilize to help single Jews meet other single Jews. By plugging-in the JDate information listed above into the Facebook search engine, you may even find other eligible bachelors and bachelorettes you never knew existed. It's surprising how many thirty-two-year-old Jewish males graduated from UCLA in 2002 and now work in high tech. Not everybody is on JDate after all, but nearly everyone is on Facebook. It's amazing how far the word "Jewish" will take you!

STATUS (UP)DATES

Facebook has changed the dating world as we know it in other ways as well. Not only do you get to "publish" who you're dating, but you can track every step from "in a relationship" to "engaged" to "married." Of course, those News Feeds include breakups, too, either by changing your relationship status back to "single" or even changing your last name in the case of a divorce. Facebook has replaced the rumor mill—or perhaps made it worse! It was a shocker when I found out via the networking website that two separate friends of mine broke off their respective engagements.

What's more awkward is when the Facebook News Feed informs you that your exes have moved on. It doesn't matter how long ago a relationship ended, who ended it, or how it ended—it's never easy to learn that your ex has met someone new. It's even harder when your entire mutual world finds out about it along with you. And of course, it's an entirely other level of devastating when your status is still listed as "single."

Facebook was how I found out an ex-boyfriend, Nate, was selling his business and moving to a small town across the country. After a quick look at his profile page, I was able to quickly figure out he was moving to be with a girl . . . a non-Jewish girl. For some reason that irked me because this was the same guy who told me that one of the reasons he loved me so much was because I was Jewish, was active in the Jewish community, and shared the same Jewish values. I guess those qualities weren't so important to him after all.

Facebook was also how I learned about another ex getting hitched. Suddenly, Greg's profile went from "single" to "married," and I didn't even know he was dating anyone! After a phone call to a mutual friend, I found out he broke up with me for the woman who is now his wife. And it was just a few short months after he broke up with me that he proposed to her. Greg was the same guy who told me he wasn't ready to get married because he had recently broken off an engagement. His new wife is Jewish, but pictures showed the bride wearing a sleeveless dress to their chuppah-less wedding, which was performed by a Rent-a-Rabbi. Did I mention that lobster was served at the reception? The same (and might I add, informative) mutual friend told me that Greg didn't think the prewedding relationship classes required by most Rabbis were necessary. That was the part that irked me the most. Wear whatever wedding dress you want, serve whatever food you want, but meeting with the Rabbi is an important step especially when you already have one broken engagement under your belt.

The worst Facebook shock I've gotten was an engagement announcement posted by Sam. Sam and I met on JDate a few years ago while he was in the process of moving to Los Angeles. We spent hours talking on the phone, but just before we met I decided, unbeknownst to Sam, that he shouldn't move to a new city and immediately enter a new relationship. Thus, the first date was excruciatingly awkward and ruined any hope of a future. We later became friends and even made a pact we would start a family together if we were both single in ten years. So I was definitely bummed when my backup put a rock on another girl's finger.

If I sound bitter it's because that's how I felt back then when I read all three of these status updates within the same month. I felt as though I could make any guy commit, just not to me. All a guy has to do was date me, and the next thing you know they found their beshert . . . with the next girl. So I decided to look at it with a positive spin: I had done three mitzvahs. I broke Nate's heart, turning him off to all Jewish girls and driving him to the opposite coast to find Kristen. I was Greg's rebound from his broken engagement, readying him to meet and marry Sharon. And I pushed Sam away and into the arms of Lisa. I feel like I was instrumental in bringing three couples together. Too bad I wasn't their official Shadchan, otherwise I'd have earned my ticket to heaven!

INTERNET INNOVATION

An email is circulating in the Jewish community and it looks like a chain letter at first, but it is actually a very interesting request from a man looking for a wife. Like a chain letter, the email was sent to me by a friend, who had forwarded the email from another friend, who had received it from another friend. The letter was from a single Jewish man asking his friends and friends of his friends and their friend's friends (you get the idea) to set him up. He said he was really serious about finding his beshert and getting married, and he would reward whomever set him up with his future wife with a trip to anywhere in the world. I thought the email was genius. What better way than to promote yourself and your pursuit of your beshert than through today's most popular form of communication?

If this sounds like something you'd want to do, keep these considerations in mind: Since this email is basically a marketing ploy, use the space wisely. In no more than one page, describe yourself honestly (including your faults) and describe the type of person you're looking to meet, listing just a few requirements and plenty of preferences. If you have the funds or connections, go ahead and offer something in return. This is, after all, your future spouse someone could be setting you up with, and a nice dinner or a monetary reward is not much in the big scheme of things.

Email everyone you know and ask that they forward the letter on to all their contacts, and so on and so forth. Post the letter on your Facebook account and basically pimp yourself out. Stop relying on just JDate and mixers, simply hoping your friends will think of you and take action when they meet a great single guy or gal. This is your future love life we're talking about here, so take the reins and get typing.

Use every tool to your advantage. Combine the powers of JDate, Facebook, and email to help you find your beshert. In that same token, make sure you don't have anything embarrassing posted on Facebook or Instagram or any other social networking site, whether it be a photo, a meme, a comment thread, or what have you. As Facebook continues to change their settings, they are exposing old threads that were once private. Not anymore. Now you have to go through your timeline one month at a time and the annoying Facebook graph app one page at a time until you hide, delete, or untag yourself from anything that shouldn't be public. Additionally, you need to adjust your privacy settings so that people can find you but can't see your private posts and photos until you've added them as friends. Once you've set up security precautions both for your safety as well as your peace of mind, you can effectively and productively date using every Internet tool.

....

♥ Julie

Julie was recently at a mixer and was asked by two separate men for her information. So she gave her business card to them both, but she failed to write her personal cell phone number or email address on the back. I told her for future reference, she should scribble her personal info on the back of her card so the guy knows she's really interested and not just giving out her card as a polite form of rejection. Luckily, both guys sent an email to her work account at the beginning of the week.

The first one (whose name I can't even remember because he was so inconsequential) only asked about work. After the second email exchange, he finally came out with his real motivation for writing: He had been recently laid off and wanted to know if her law firm was hiring. I advised her to curtly reply that they were not and to not write anything to prolong the conclusion of the conversation. This guy was a dud, and, although he may have been nice enough, he wasn't worth the time or effort to keep in touch with as he had ulterior motives when he showed interest in her.

The second one, Josh, seemed friendly and interested. He asked her about real estate, since she recently bought her condo, and about the big Jewish mixer coming up she was helping to organize. They traded emails all week, and she typed her personal cell phone number in a subtle way under her signature each time. Finally, at the end of the week and after a dozen emails, he asked if they could get together . . . to talk about real estate. I wasn't ready to write him off as a dud quite yet; I figured he could have been making up an excuse to get together because he was insecure or feared rejection. But when he did finally call, he rang her on her office phone, blatantly ignoring her cell phone number (when she told me this, the term "dud" started flashing before my eyes). Unfortunately they couldn't get their schedules to sync up, and he said he would call next week to try again, but he never did.

Two weeks later, I advised Julie to send him a quick and casual email letting him know she'd been really busy but that her schedule had finally slowed down. He replied via email twenty-four hours later—which was a good sign—but once again it was about real estate and he didn't make any move to make plans—not a good sign. I was ready to write this guy off once and for all as a dud. I couldn't understand why he even bothered replying. When she finally decided to type his name into the Facebook search bar, she found him easily since they had some mutual friends. But upon clicking on his profile, she found that although his relationship status was nonexistent, there were numerous photos of him with the same girl in very, shall we say, "friendly" postures. This dude was in fact a total dud.

How and when Julie and other singles should write off a dude as a dud is not always obvious. The former possible suitor was easy to identify as a dud, but the latter suitor, Josh, didn't make it easy to decide at first. Use a mixture of your instinct and any evident signs to know when to stop wasting your time and move on. If a dude doesn't call after a few emails when he has your phone number, he's a dud. If he only discusses subjects that benefit him, he's a dud. If a gal has ulterior motives, she can be labeled a dud, too. She can also be a dud if she doesn't return phone calls or avoids making plans. If it's too difficult, it may very well just not be worth it, and it's time to cut your losses before you invest any more time or energy and move on.

♥ Natalie

Party girl Natalie takes tons of photos when she's out at night and posts them all to Instagram, which is linked to her Facebook account. She even updates her JDate photos each time she reactivates her account after each fleeting relationship. All her friends comment about her wild ways and how sexy she looks. There are random girls and guys in each photo, sometimes she's hanging on the guys, and sometimes she looks like she's celebrating her twenty-first birthday rather than her thirty-first—not because she looks so young but because she hasn't slowed down and parties hard.

I implored upon Natalie to untag or delete many of the photos and to stop freely posting while she is out and in the moment. I explained she was sending the wrong message and attracting the wrong type of guy. Of course she can find a man who wants to continue to have a great time on the town with her, but she also needs to find one who doesn't think she drinks every night or hooks up with random guys or doesn't take life seriously, because that is not who she is. I know that, and she knows that, but that's not the image she is putting out there. Natalie needs to clean up her social networking sites, and, while she can still go out and have fun, she needs to keep it offline.

 ## Mike

Mike is the total opposite of Natalie. Mike doesn't post anything on his Facebok page, but he does scroll through and see what everyone else is doing all day long. There is nothing too personal on his Facebook page, so no prospect can decipher much. If you click on his Friends link you will see many, many women of all ages, and the younger ones are dressed quite provocatively in their profile photos. The

HOW TO WOO A JEW

sheer number of sexy women that are his "friends" can be intimidating, and that mixed with the lack of personal information makes a prospective woman be a bit suspicious. Some of that time Mike spends perusing Facebook should instead be spent cleaning out his friends list. He's a thirty-three-year-old man; does he really need to be Facebook friends with dozens and dozens of girls in their early twenties whom he doesn't even really know but randomly parties with sometimes?

Everyone ought to regularly clean out his or her Friends list, as the company you keep is an indication of who you are as well. I don't necessarily attest to "birds of a feather flock together," as it is not fair to judge someone solely by their friends, let alone their Facebook friends, because people tend to add acquaintances without a second glance. Mike, though, is not a twenty-one-year-old party girl anymore than Natalie is. If Mike wants a woman to take him seriously, then he needs to take dating more seriously.

 Lauren

Lauren has mainly used Facebook as a place to share photos of her kids with family and friends around the world, but now she wants to use it more socially. After her divorce, she spent a long time adjusting her profile to that of a single mother's. It was a few months into the separation before she hid her relationship status, and then a few months longer until she removed "married" even though her relationship status was still hidden. And it wasn't until a few months after her divorce that she changed her name on Facebook back to her maiden name. Along the way, she hid or deleted lovey-dovey photos of her and her ex-husband together.

Lauren gets how Facebook can affect her dating life. She makes sure there are plenty of photos of her by herself and with her girlfriends to balance out the ones of her with her kids and of her kids alone. She doesn't want prospective dates to think that she is "only" a Mom and doesn't have a life outside her kids. Although Lauren is still exploring JDate and how that works, she understands how Facebook can help or hurt her dating life. She already made sure her JDate profile picture and Facebook profile photo are the same and saved the cute photo of her kids for her Facebook time line.

 ## Beth

Beth took my advice about writing her pitch letter to send to family and friends. She described herself as a woman who is "forty-eight years young . . . educated, successful in her career, friendly, outgoing and smart, while at the same time quiet and sensitive and shy, who has everything going for her except a partner in life. Loves having so many nieces and nephews, loves traveling, good wine, and live music, loves being outdoors and being active, and would love to share this all with someone as well as learn to love some new hobbies and interests!"

Beth went on to admit to being a little too picky along the way but has now realized what's important in life—it's not what she thought ten years ago. Though she still wants a woman relatively close to her age and with a career, she cares more about the woman being passionate about her

HOW TO WOO A JEW

career rather than successful, she doesn't care if the woman is divorced or has children but simply wants someone who loves family in general.

Beth implored her family and friends to think about who they know and to feel free to forward her email to anyone else who may know someone. Because she is an artist, she offered to waive her commission fee to create a personal painting for whoever succeeded in finding her beshert.

 ## David

David doesn't want to use any technology for dating because it doesn't feel authentic to him. He has a Facebook account but rarely posts anything. A lot of people used it as a way to send their condolences when his wife died, so many of his Facebook friends are somehow connected to his late wife. David doesn't see how Facebook can be romantic whatsoever and would rather send a handwritten note than an email. Again, he is tech-savvy and even has a smartphone, but he finds communicating that way cold and impersonal. As such, he also doesn't want a woman who is overly obsessed with Facebook either.

It took David one year after his wife's death to change his relationship status from married to single. There are still photos of her on his profile, and he is not planning on removing them; any woman coming into his life is going to have to be okay with her photographic presence. A few years ago, David changed his profile picture to one of just himself (chosen with the help of his daughters), and he is accepting friend requests from women he meets, but he's still not using Facebook for dating at this point. David's approach isn't a bad one, but eventually he will have to accept that Facebook is here to stay and he may have to become more active online as he dates more actively.

....

HOW TO WOO A JEW

Chapter 8

⬟ FIRST DATES ❥

FIRST DATES CAN BE nerve-racking. Are you dressed right? Will you recognize the other person from JDate? Will you have anything to discuss? Will there be chemistry? Do you have food in your teeth? Will you split the bill? Will there be a first kiss? Does your breath smell? Will this be your last first date? These and so many more anxiety-ridden thoughts go through everyone's minds on all first dates.

MAKING PLANS

You've already had your first phone call, during which you made plans. Your date will either be a midweek date or it'll be during Prime Time Date Night (Friday or Saturday night). Don't take it personally at this point if you didn't get a PTDN; treat a first date the same regardless of what night it is on. It's nice when the date-maker takes the initiative and asks if there's any food the prospect is allergic to or any specific food or restaurant that he or she hates.

Then, based on the answer, offer to make a reservation and say that you will call your date back soon to inform her or him of the where and when. The date-maker should then go ahead and pick a middle-of-the road restaurant: not too expensive, not a chain, and not too fancy or too casual. Then, the day before the date, the date-maker would make another really great impression by calling and letting the prospect know where you two will be eating and what time you will be meeting there (or, possibly, taking the plunge and offering to pick up the prospect, such a brave and yet impressive move!).

When you're making plans for a date—whether you're doing the asking or being asked—it's imperative you be flexible. If she suggests sushi, don't make a gagging noise. If he suggests coffee or drinks rather than a meal, don't sigh. If she suggests the newest, trendiest, most expensive restaurant, don't roll your eyes. And if he suggests a midweek date, don't grunt or guffaw. Being flexible is an admirable and sought-after quality. It doesn't mean you're desperate for a date anytime or anywhere but rather that you're open to trying new things and willing to compromise—traits that people often desire in a mate.

Sure, lots of us ladies love a guy who tells us to get dressed up to go out on Saturday night—Prime Time Date Night—to a fancy-shmancy restaurant where he can impress us with the fact that he was able to finagle reservations. But hopefully, a gal will feel just as comfortable and excited to be in jeans at the greasy but delicious hole-in-the-wall neighborhood joint on a Thursday night because your date knows that's when they have a special and delicious delicatessen not normally on the menu.

If it's your first phone conversation and you're discussing your date plans, the last thing you want to do is come across as snobby or inflexible by hemming and hawing over every suggestion. If it's

    HOW TO WOO A JEW

a second or third date and you know her favorite food is sushi, then take her there even if it means you order an overpriced teriyaki chicken dinner. Just don't make an icky face or yucky noise when the raw fish arrives at your table. There's something you can order everywhere you go even if it's just the house salad with grilled chicken, so there's no need to be difficult by rejecting every restaurant suggestion your date makes.

If you're that person who is sensitive to this, that, and the other—you have a nut allergy, a gluten intolerance, and you're a vegetarian—then you need to make first dates with a list of restaurants in mind that you know you can eat in.

You can take turns picking the place as you and your prospect continue to date—if one restaurant is a flop, you'll be able to tease your date from then on. If you're making plans via email or instant messenger, it's even more important to not make a sarcastic comment about the food or the service or what have you because so much gets lost in translation online. "LOL" only gets you so far. Don't be a doormat—if you ate Chinese food last night and don't want it again, it's okay to say so. Some couples will bond over both being food snobs, but, for the most part, nobody wants dinner to turn into restaurant wars—this is the situation where you want to be easy and not a challenge.

I'm a people-watcher by nature and a dating expert by trade, which means I observe many couples on dates for entertainment's sake and take notes for professional sake. Here are some things I've learned from being an outside observer:

AWKWARD SILENCES

At some point during a first date there comes a time when there's an awkward silence. This is the time when the stereotypical, and often negative, trait of Jewish women comes in handy as something positive. Most first daters are full of nerves and are scared of the awkward silence, thus the incessant talking and persistent inquiring by Jewish women can also be invoked by a man to keep the flow.

We've all met the "incessant talkers" who talk about themselves so much that just about anyone could be sitting across from them. They don't even realize they aren't asking you questions or that you have the tuned-out, bored look on your face because they are so self-involved and egocentric. The incessant talker doesn't even realize they've been monopolizing the conversation or that you haven't been able to get a word in edgewise; they gab about anything, go off on tangents, and barely stop chatting long enough to eat. And if you're on a date with an incessant talker, then they will probably leave the date thinking it went well, not aware they didn't learn anything new about you or involve you whatsoever. The incessant talker thinks they're being positive and upbeat and thinks they're doing the date a favor by not letting a moment of silence fall upon their table. Make sure you're not an incessant talker.

We've also all sat across from the "persistent inquirers" who ask so many questions that they don't even give you a chance to get to know them. They're so concerned with filling every second with conversation that their efforts come off as overly eager and insincere. The persistent inquirer asks textbook questions and makes you feel as if you're on a job interview because, though they ask the questions, they don't give you the opportunity to show interest in them, they don't let the answers turn into a conversation, and they aren't really listening to the answers at all. If you're on a date with a persistent inquirer, then they will probably leave the date thinking it went well, not aware you didn't learn anything about them. Just like the incessant talker, the persistent inquirers think they're being positive and upbeat and that they're doing the date a favor by not letting a moment of silence fall upon their table. Make sure you're not a persistent inquirer.

These types are trying to be helpful and considerate, but they're also nervous and scared. It doesn't help that not everyone is known for their communication skills, but no one wants to be on a date when it feels like you're pulling teeth, trying to carry on a conversation with someone who gives one-word answers, doesn't ask questions, and tends to get distracted easily. So rather than getting annoyed by the incessant talker or the persistent inquirer's attempts at making the date less than awkward, appreciate the lack of awkward silences instead.

Unless one of you enjoys being a blabbermouth and the other is more the silent type, then this arrangement won't work. Instead, let the date breathe like a fine wine and give your date a chance to show you that he or she is interested. Even if one person makes a little less of an effort at chitchat and the other person is forced to make a little more of an effort, the conversation will still hopefully end up having the right tempo. By the way, awkward silences aren't always so bad, because, if by chance the silence ends up not being so awkward, you may have found your match. You need to find someone that you will still want to talk to fifty years from now, but it's just as important you find someone you can comfortably sit in silence with as well.

FLIRTING

First-date flirting will become an art form to you if it hasn't already. The key is to let your date know you're interested without giving off the wrong signals. The main thing is to maintain eye contact, listen to what your date is saying, and react appropriately. That means smile, laugh, nod, or frown according to the topic. Smiling and laughing are the most important signals, which, in conjunction with eye contact, let your date know you are having a good time. If you're sitting across from each other, then reach over the table and place your hand over your date's, or extend your leg under the table so that your foot is touching his or hers. If you're sitting next to each other, then place your hand on his or her arm or leg when something humorous is said and you laugh. Turn your body toward your date and keep your body language open, which means do not cross your arms over your chest and if you cross your legs then cross them toward your date.

LET'S GIVE THEM SOMETHING TO TALK ABOUT

What do you talk about on a first date? And what topics are off the table, literally? You're going out on a first date with this person because you either met on JDate or met out and about or were set up. No matter how you met, you will know a certain amount of information about each other. Here are some things to consider based on how you met your date:

JDate and Other Dating Websites: If you met online, then you know a lot about each other already due to your respective profile answers. This is the information you would normally be exchanging on the first date had you met out and about or were set up by someone.

So try not to reveal too much more about yourself because you might be exchanging third-date personal information on a first date, before you even know if there will be a third date. But how do you do that when you already know so much about each other? Take the basic information provided and ask questions to expand upon it. You know your date has a college degree, so ask where he or she went to college. You know your date has a dog, so ask what kind. You know your date is in advertising, but what exactly does he or she do? Basically, you should expand upon the information provided without digging too deep. Stick to typical first-date conversation topics. Learn from my mistake: I went on my first JDate not long after signing up, and, since we already knew so much about each other from our profiles, we ended up having a much deeper conversation than you typically would with someone who is still, theoretically, a stranger. I felt such a bond with this guy even though we had just been on one date simply because I divulged private things about myself and he confided in me as well. By the second date I was thinking way too far ahead and considering him in a much more serious capacity than where our relationship realistically stood. When there wasn't a third date, I was devastated even though there were a multitude of reasons why we weren't a match because I was stuck remembering how much we shared. From then on I learned to hold back a bit and reminded myself that first dates were just surface get-to-know-you opportunities, not times to exchange secrets and intimate stories.

Out and About: If you met this way, you probably don't know much about each other except for the information you exchanged at the birthday party, bar, mixer, or work function, which is typically kept to the basics of age, occupation, location, and what brought you to that venue on that night. This means you have carte blanche to discuss typical first-date topics. If you get stuck, then think of the questions JDate asks you for your profile: Where did you go to school? What did you study? Where did you grow up? What temple do you go to?

Setups and Blind Dates: These are the first dates you enter into knowing the least about each other since you have never met before and did not get to vet each other's online profile. Chances are the matchmaker showed you a photo of each other and told you a few basic details. Then you either contacted each other and scheduled a date or the matchmaker did so on your behalf. Either way, you have a lot of ground to cover on the first date. It will usually begin with a "How do you know [the person who set you up]?" and then parlay into a "Remind me how old you are, what you do, and where you live," which should organically turn into the more detailed "Where did you grow up? Where did you go to school?" and so on.

You can always play Jewish Geography and figure out who you know in common, but tread lightly as that game will inevitably bring up names to which one of you will have a negative reaction. As discussed in Chapter 3, Do the Jew, everyone knows everyone, or at least knows someone who knows someone. Do not, I repeat, DO NOT, talk badly about anyone regardless of your history. First of all, when you badmouth someone, it reflects badly upon you. Second of all, the Jewish community in each city is relatively small, and word tends to spread quickly. Finally, DO NOT discuss your past relationship history on a first date.

Oftentimes, the question "Why are you still single?" arises on a first date when someone is impressed by how awesome you are. This should be flattering, and there is a correct way to answer (and there are many incorrect ways to answer). The best thing to say is, "I haven't found the right person yet," and leave it at that. If you are really into your date, then say that line while you look directly into his or her eyes. And then say, "What about you? Why are you still single?" Chances are you will hear an identical response to the one you gave, and hopefully both of you will smile and get that tingly feeling.

CHECK, PLEASE!

In addition to awkward silences, there is that awkward moment when the check arrives. On my best first date ever, my date (now my fiancé) excused himself to use the bathroom and slipped the waitress his credit card on his way so that we didn't have to endure that uncomfortable moment. Otherwise, both people should make the effort to pay and be ready to split the bill. Of course, it's always a generous gesture when the man waves away the woman's offer, but, if he does accept the motion to go Dutch, don't automatically write him off as uninterested. Many men are so used to women assuming they will pay that sometimes they will test a woman to see if she is faking the move to her purse or if she means it. When the man does pay, the woman can show appropriate appreciation by saying thank you right then.

If the date was awful (and remember, it could have been awful in your mind but not in the mind of your date, so tread lightly), then insist on paying for yourself. No one wants to feel indebted to a bad date; pay your way, thank your date for his or her time, and leave with dignity.

CELL PHONES

The worst way technology affects dating is that people are tempted to use phones during a date. Never, ever answer your phone during a first, second, or third date! In fact, put the phone on silent: no beeping, no vibrating, no ringing. Don't even look at the darn thing if you are even remotely interested in the person you're on a date with! Dates should be cell-phone-free zones, where handheld devices should be banished, checked at the door with your coat, or, better yet, left in the car. You're taking the time and effort to go on the date, so give it your full attention and remember that you deserve and should expect the same in return. That said, if you have kids or a sick parent then keep your phone on a low ring volume and on vibrate just in case of emergencies and let your date know in advance so that he or she doesn't think you're being rude.

I will admit, I once accepted a date even though I had a feeling ahead of time that it wasn't going to work out, so I scheduled my friend to call me about twenty minutes into the date. When I arrived to the restaurant and had my suspicions confirmed, I then set up a realistic situation for the emergency phone call. I told my date that I had been helping my best friend, her husband, and their one-year-old daughter move that day, which was true. Twenty minutes later, my BFF called to tell me that her hubby had accidentally bashed his finger with a hammer and needed to be taken to the emergency room, and she asked if I would mind coming back immediately to watch the baby. Of course I said yes and then hurriedly relayed the fake phone call while gathering up my things and offering to pay for my drink before thanking him for picking up the tab. Extreme? Possibly. But I didn't want to hurt his feelings.

SAYING GOODBYE

Saying goodbye is probably more awkward than saying hello. If you don't want to see the person again, then figuring out how to leave the date without a brutal rejection and without leading the person on can be tricky. The best way to do so is to give a warm and respectful hug and say, "Thank you for a nice evening." And if your date offers to call you then say, "You know, I had a nice time but I don't think it's a good idea. I just don't want to waste either of our time, you know?"

If you are interested and you've given all the signals that you're interested and you've read all the signals and believe your date is interested, then there shouldn't be a problem. If you arrived separately, then the man should walk the woman to her car or her subway stop and give her a sweet, three-second, closed-mouth kiss and tell her he looks forward to seeing her again soon. If the man picked the woman up, then he should walk her to her door and give her that sweet, three-second, closed-mouth kiss on the porch. Both parties need to have open and welcoming body language so that the other feels comfortable making a move.

If you are interested in seeing where this connection could go in the future, then leave it at that. As excited as you are at the prospect of something more and as turned on as you might be, I urge you not to take it past the kiss. Many people have had the experience of being so enamored by the date and the chemistry of the first kiss that the first date ends with sex. Sometimes the date turns into a relationship, and sometimes it ends up becoming a one-night stand. You never know what is going to happen, but you do know that you are looking for your beshert and not another notch on your bedpost. Want this time, this date, this person to be different? Then leave it with the kiss on the porch.

You're going to go on lots of first dates and very few second dates and even fewer third dates. Some of the first dates will be terrible, some will end in a one-night stand, some will end with a kiss and a hope for a second date that never comes, and some will end with a kiss and be followed by the phone call and the second date. You have to keep going on each first date with a positive attitude and hedge your bets that this could in fact be your last first date.

But before you go on your last first date, you're going to have to accept or ask out more first dates then you thought you'd ever go on when you were an innocent teenager fantasizing about falling in love. Accept EVERY first date you're asked out on because you never know who you're going to meet. It's one thing if you absolutely, positively know the other person is not right for you whatsoever, but, if you're not sure, then give the person the benefit of the doubt and say yes. It's not fair not to accept a date just because there wasn't instant attraction, nor is it fair to judge a potential date based on what you don't have in common. Focus on the positives: the things you have in common or the glowing recommendation from a mutual friend. If you're open to meeting anyone at anytime, you'll probably end up getting asked out on a lot more dates. And if after one date you decide to part amicably, then you'll at least have met a new friend who can now introduce you to their friends . . . and of course you can return the favor!

This advice doesn't simply mean hoping an unsuccessful date will lead to a delightful date with one of the original prospect's friends; you have to create opportunities for yourself by keeping that open mind-set in every situation because you may meet someone when you least expect it. I know a number of couples who met at shivas. That's right; they met because someone died. It may seem odd to even think of checking out the crowd at a shiva, but I'm sure the person who passed away would be happy to know their death resulted in a simcha. In fact, in the case of one of the couples, the host of the shiva (the daughter of the woman who died) later hosted the couple's engagement party.

You really never know when you're going to meet someone, so it's important to be open and willing to accept a first date at all times. I was on a first date that was set up by my mom and the guy's mom without even the exchange of photos. The date was a dud for me, but I knew he would be perfect for one of my friends. I made sure my body language and the way I ended the conversation would make it clear that I wasn't interested in him. He still called two days later, and, although I was flattered, I decided to let him know my plan. I told him that I enjoyed getting to know him but that I thought he would be better with my friend than with me, and I asked if he would be interested in meeting her. Luckily he said yes, and I got to create a shidduch! Because my friend has heard me tout my "accept every first date" advice, she was willing to go on a date with someone I had also been on a date with, and now they are in a committed relationship.

....

 ## Julie

A new JDate match for Julie usually means a new problem she needs help with. But this time the match was going well. Julie met Matt on JDate and gave him her number after just a few emails, and he called immediately to make plans. So far so good, right?

Matt asked Julie out for drinks after work at a restaurant that's known for its fun happy hour with live music. I thought it was a good choice, but Julie was already complaining about not being asked out for Saturday-night dinner. I told Julie that midweek casual dates for drinks is the norm for first dates nowadays because people don't want to make a huge time commitment before they're sure the other person is worth it. I get it—I may not have liked it when I was in her shoes, but I get it. I pumped Julie up for the date, she changed her attitude, and she was off on her merry way.

The date turned out to be a huge success, and Matt asked her out for another date before the night was over. Huge plus and major brownie points! But, as awesome as the date seemed to go, he asked her out for yet another midweek date. This time, I was perplexed. I asked Julie if they had any conversations pertaining to scheduling, and she remembered mentioning attending bachelorette and birthday parties for the next few weekends. She also re-membered him saying he had plans to visit his parents in the Midwest. So again, I calmly reassured her that this sounded like he was trying to make plans sooner rather than later, and she agreed.

So at the end of the second date, when he asked her out for a Sunday afternoon, she was bordering on livid. This time I had no excuse or explanation for her. He obviously liked her and wanted to keep seeing her and getting to know her, but why was he not asking her out for a Saturday night—Prime Time Date Night? Some guys see Prime Time Date Night as a night for people who are in relationships. But by the third date, it simply doesn't make sense, and, unless there's a schedule conflict, there's no longer any valid excuse. So, I advised Julie to accept the Sunday date with an open mind and told her that when he mentions the next date, she needs to simply interject nicely and tell him she has a really busy week ahead of her but that she's available on Saturday. If he doesn't get the hint, then the blunt truth Julie needs to face is that he probably is dating other people and has already given the Prime Time Date Night slot to someone else. That's a tough fact to swallow, but Julie needs to understand it's the current reality of dating and that she should be filling her dance card, too. And if she stills wants to date him after that, I don't see the harm, but she should proceed with caution.

♥ Natalie

Natalie has been going out on lots of first dates. Some are horrendous, some are fun, and some are promising. But Natalie keeps falling for the same lines, just in different formats, and getting burned. She doesn't want a guy to tell her he's successful; she wants to actually hear about his career and see things in his day-to-day life that speak to his lifestyle, accomplishments, and ambitions. Yet she continuously falls prey to men exaggerating their success. One guy she met last summer told her he had to take trips to Dallas, Chicago, New York, and Los Angeles by the end of that year. It turns out the trip to New York was to see friends, the vacation to Los Angeles never happened, and the two other trips were actually one trip with two stops. Here she thought he was some jet-setter, but he was just good at making himself out to be bigger than he was. The truth came out soon enough, but, until then, she had allowed him to build himself up in her mind.

Another guy told Natalie all about the fancy trips he took and the expensive hotels he stayed in and his exciting staycations. He dressed impeccably and always took her to fancy restaurants. This guy wasn't lying about his lifestyle, but it was a lifestyle afforded to him because he was single and didn't have anyone else to take care of. He was financially responsible, with low mortgage payments on his condo and a healthy savings, but his lifestyle and his salary didn't calculate to support a wife or a family. Those trips and staycations would fall by the wayside once he got married and became a father. Natalie shouldn't have to be suspicious all the time, but she should listen critically and ask questions that will help her figure out the truth without sounding like a crazy, gold-digging stalker. In neither of these specific examples were the men lying to her; they were just representing themselves in the best light, which is what everyone does. It's a matter of trusting your instinct, and, when that fails, you need to rely on questions to dig a little deeper.

 ## Mike

Mike went out with a girl, Amanda, from JDate whom he contacted using his hidden profile. He and Amanda had been communicating for a while and finally decided to meet after exchanging flirtatious emails. They made plans for Saturday night at a dive bar where the crowd wouldn't be too busy and the music wouldn't be too loud. Mike arrived promptly at nine o'clock, and almost immediately his cell phone rang. Amanda was calling to say she was running really late—she was coming from dinner at her parent's and she not only underestimated how long it would take to drive across town but had also run into traffic. She was apologetic and called a few more times to update him on her whereabouts and ETA. After thirty minutes of waiting, Mike left without telling her.

As harsh as it sounds that Mike left the bar when Amanda was hastily trying to get there, I think he did the right thing.

Thirty minutes is enough, even though she was calling, as her being late was rude and a waste of his time. I told him if she were to call and continue to be apologetic and want another date, he should accept and mercilessly tease her about taking advantage of Jewish Standard Time (JST) when they finally met. Since she did in fact call a few times to let him know she was running late and sounded genuinely apologetic, he should without a doubt give her a second chance. I told Mike it wouldn't have been the end of the world had he shelved his pride and impatience and waited fifteen more minutes, since she was updating him, but I also understood why he did what he did.

We all have cell phones nowadays, so there is absolutely no excuse why someone can't call and inform you if he or she will be late prior to the date. If a date doesn't respect you enough to call, then no second chance should be given, as it shouldn't matter what the excuse is. Amanda did call Mike after she finally got to the dive bar, an hour late, and although she was disappointed, she understood why he left. They made plans to meet up the next day for brunch, so it was no longer Prime Time Date Night, but it was the very next day and they didn't lose the momentum by pretending to be too busy to get together.

 ## Lauren

Lauren has been on a few dates with Seth, who is a divorced father, but Lauren cannot forget what happened on their first date: they had their first kiss in public, and Seth copped a feel, brushing her breast with his hand deliberately yet subtly, and it made her feel very uncomfortable. She has continued to date him and even likes him. Their kids have met during a playdate, and she thinks they're a great match and could even see a future with him. But she was so embarrassed after that first date, and she doesn't understand why he would touch her that way on purpose in the middle of their first kiss. He hasn't done anything weird since, and she really wants to get over it but is having a hard time doing so. She wants to know how to move on so they can get more serious. The act obviously wasn't bad enough for her to turn down his request for a second and third and fourth date (and fifth and sixth), so why is she still harping on it? It's time to put it to rest.

Unfortunately for Seth, you can only make a first impression once, but fortunately for him (and unbeknownst to him), Lauren has conceded by seeing him for the past six weeks. My advice to Lauren is to tell him, in a joking tone, that he should never do that again and let him know, teasingly, that he should know how lucky he was she gave him a second chance. She should allow him to respond and then drop the topic, forget about it, and start making new memories to replace that one awful one. If she really wants something with this guy, she needs to confront the situation head-on.

Lauren also needs to remember people are often extremely nervous on first dates, want desperately to make a good impression, and therefore can make complete fools out of themselves instead. Seth was probably excited and forgot to mind his manners for a brief moment. If Lauren wants to make this work she has to chalk his behavior up to first-date jitters and excuse the act. When you're not the nervous one, it's easy to forget how nervous the other person might be. Ultimately you have to weigh your pros and cons when deciding if you're going to continue seeing the prospect. But remember, aren't people allowed to make mistakes?

In Lauren's case, Seth's behavior wasn't bad enough to cause her to stop accepting his dates, so what is Lauren afraid of? Does she think he's going to do something else that embarrasses her in public or move too fast for her sexually? Is she thinking he has tried this on other first dates? Is she afraid that was his true self? Or is she just looking for some kind of fault in him so she can put up her guard and stop herself from possibly getting hurt? Before Lauren answers any of these questions, she needs to casually confront Seth and then question herself to see why she might be intentionally ruining a good thing.

 ## Beth

Beth had an awful day yesterday, and, in turn, it possibly ruined her promising date last night. The day started off with a bang, literally. Someone began setting off illegal fireworks in the street at 3:00 AM, waking Beth up. After finally falling back asleep an hour later, Beth slept through her alarm, and by the time she was up and ready she was running late for work. After driving forty-five minutes in rush-hour traffic, she arrived at her meeting to find out it had been canceled, at which point she realized she had absentmindedly left her phone on silent and never got the call. Finally, when she got back home, there was a message waiting for her from an owner of one of the art studios where she both works and shows her pieces. He wanted her to come and see him. He didn't say what the meeting was about, and Beth became very nervous and started biting her freshly manicured nails.

At the studio, the owner told Beth he needed to push her next show back a few months, so she became even more aggravated and chewed her way through ten nails worth of polish. She made her way to lunch after the meeting, but her order was delivered wrong—except of course she didn't discover it until it was too late—and then she got a text from her mother telling her a close family relative was in the hospital. *Whew!*

After all that, Beth finished working for the day, and she had to run home to freshen up for the date she had previously been extremely excited about but now was dreading. She had thought about canceling but never found time during the day to call, so now she was stuck going on the date and was in a terrible mood, with no energy and barely enough time to roll on some fresh deodorant. Beth called me on her way, and I gave her a pep talk. I reminded her how excited she was about this prospect—her qualities, hobbies, and looks, all of which she was attracted to. I told her to start with faking a smile while she was talking to me, since smiling sends a message to your brain that you're happy and this will cause a negative mind-set to turn positive. By the time she arrived at the restaurant I think she was in a better mood, but it still wasn't going to be the best representation of who she is.

So what can you do when you're having a bad day and are supposed to go on a first date (or any date)? You can try and reschedule—simply call early enough in the day, explain that your day is sucking and you want to be at your best for the date, and see if he or she is available later that week. If you can't reschedule for anytime soon, let your date know you'd rather see him or her sooner than later, so you'll turn your mood around and look forward to the date ending your day on a better note. If, like Beth, it's too late to reschedule, then try to at least see if you can push back the time of the date so you can go home and freshen up, maybe take a quick soak in the tub to decompress, and change your clothes. Try to separate business from pleasure, and remember: Your life partner is going to have to support you through thick and thin, so there's no reason to pretend your life is perfect. Try to keep your description of your bad day to a minimum and get back to getting to know each other by discussing fun, positive topics.

David

David is reviving chivalry all on his own. His late wife was an independent woman who was able to allow him to feel like The Man while at the same time was able to feel confident that she could do everything, though she wanted his help. She allowed him to change lightbulbs, kill spiders, carry luggage, and take out the trash, and he enjoyed taking care of her. Now that David is dating, he likes to pick up women for dates and he likes to open doors for them. He even prefers to pay for dinner, and, though he appreciates it when a woman offers to pay, especially when he knows she's being genuine, he never accepts even if the date was terrible. He wants to make a woman feel special regardless whether he wants a second date or not.

David does all of this organically and doesn't want his date to think it's forced. He once met a woman who used an obvious sales tactic on him, which was a major turnoff. Anytime David called he heard, "Hi, David!" Every time he answered her call he heard, "Hi, David!" When she left a voice mail it was, "Hi, David!" Each and every text message read, "Hi, David!" David felt like it was just too much, too over the top. The woman was obviously using a sales technique she learned to help remember names and make the person she was talking to feel special, but instead it had the opposite effect and came off as insincere.

David was turned off on another date when the prospect rudely informed the waitress her order was wrong and then tried to persuade David to leave a small tip because she thought the wrong order equated to bad service. In fact, David left more than 20 percent because he felt so bad about how his date mistreated the waitress. Another date appalled him when she lacked simple table manners: She didn't put her napkin on her lap, she chewed with her mouth open, she talked with food in her mouth, and she held her fork like a pendulum over her plate with her elbows on the table. Yet another date turned him off when she claimed to be on a detox and could only eat boiled chicken, steamed veggies, and brown rice, but, when they had met a few days earlier, she was drinking alcohol and snacking nonstop on Happy Hour appetizers. David isn't trying to be petty, and luckily he is having plenty of luck on the other dates he's gone on, but these few examples stood out to him. Being the gentleman he is, he didn't say anything to these women and continued to be polite, but part of him, his paternal side, wanted to advise them on their behavior. Luckily they were the exceptions and not the norm.

Chapter 9

 POLY-DATING

YOU WENT ON AN AWESOME first date, shared a sweet kiss at the end, and, the next day, you spoke on the phone and made plans for a second date. Exciting! Odds are you've been on dozens upon dozens of first dates and very few second dates, so this is a big deal. Don't actually make too big a deal out of it, but know it isn't the norm to have mutual attraction. How often have you gone on a first date where you knew within seconds there wasn't going to be a second date? Or where you were totally into your date and yet he or she never called back after you left a follow-up voice mail? Now that you're going on a second date, you need to reuse the preparation tips from Chapter 8, First Dates, about getting ready for this date. You also need to adhere to the same behavior tips regarding your manners on this date.

If your first date was not on Prime Time Date Night, then the second date should be. Let your date know you believe he or she is worth sacrificing one of your two weekend nights for a date. It shows you're serious, especially if you weren't willing to give up a

PTDN for the first date. If your first date was casual, then up the ante and make the second date a bit more fancy.

SECOND DATES AND SO ON

Second dates do not mean that you are suddenly in a committed relationship and can't continue being on JDate, or that you need to stop going on first dates or even stop going on other second dates. Keep your options open and continue actively dating. If you find yourself getting serious with one of your suitors, then let the others know just that. Until then, it's no one's business who, or even how many people, you're dating.

I created the term "poly-dating" after wasting many months corresponding with a guy I met on JDate who lived in another city but who was moving to town soon. I made the mistake of thinking we were in the making of a serious relationship, and, rather than going out and meeting other people in person, I chose to stay home and talk to him on the phone for hours. We had deep and meaningful conversations, we exchanged personal information, and we talked about what we wanted for our future. When we finally met and went on a date, we each soon realized it wasn't meant to be, and I was livid with myself for passing up on other potential suitors. I had ignored numerous emails and turned down a number of dates all because I thought I should be loyal to this guy whom I had only met online. Silly me. Luckily JDate keeps everything archived, and I was able to later go back and write some of the men and let them know I was available again.

From then on I went on dates left and right (remembering my own advice about accepting every date). Some were one-and-done types of dates, others progressed only to date number two, and a few developed into something more. Even then I was hesitant to stop poly-dating until I felt confident that one of the relationships was becoming more serious. When you're poly-dating, you will either lay the "I'm sorry but I've gotten serious with someone else" spiel on the other prospects, or you will be on the receiving end of said spiel. React with class and wish your former prospect luck—and mean it—because if you're poly-dating yourself, then it shouldn't sting as bad as it would have if you had put all your eggs in one basket.

But usually, you don't get blindsided. Usually you know it's coming. Usually you feel similarly and had even thought about making up another prospect just as an excuse to put an end to your agony. But most people don't want to jinx themselves by pretending to have met someone awesome. After all, your date isn't that bad, he or she is better than being alone, and who knows, maybe things will get better and the feelings will develop? You can avoid the thoughts of having to settle or inventing an imaginary prospect by poly-dating. And once you realize one person isn't worthy of your time, then you can end things with him or her and either add someone else to your rotation or concentrate on whomever is left.

As long as you're not lying to anyone about your status, then you are not doing anything wrong. Chances are, at the beginning, nobody is going to ask you if you are dating anyone else because they are, too. Eventually you may have to fess up, but, for the most part, what they don't know won't hurt them at this point. The only time you will ever feel bad is when a prospect who clearly isn't poly-dating is really into you and you are forced to break things off. Don't lead someone on when you have other prospects lined up. Cut them loose so that they can meet someone else. That's life in the single lane.

Poly-dating not only increases your chances of meeting someone but it also keeps you from falling for someone too quickly. If you're overly excited about someone you've only "met" online, then you need to be poly-dating. If you're already sounding out your names together after one date, then you need to be poly-dating. If you're still not being asked out for Prime Time Date Night after three dates and are instead sitting at home alone on a Saturday night, then you need to be poly-dating. If you're telling people you have a girlfriend or boyfriend but said girl or boy is still claiming to be single, then you need to be poly-dating.

Being a poly-dater is not being a player—you're not purposely out to hurt someone or deceive someone. But the one thing I caution against is getting promiscuous with all your suitors. Once you take a relationship to that level (see Chapter 11, Kosher Sex), it's time to call it off with all the others. If you're out to meet your future spouse, then spend your dates getting to know one another, finding out what you have in common, and seeing if you can be around each other for long periods of time and not just act on the physical chemistry. Poly-dating should be fun and carefree—don't treat your dates like job interviews or treat poly-dating like a chore because then you will come off as either desperate or a bore. Keep dating normally, just stop the habit of thinking that every first date should turn into a relationship.

CONFUSING CRUSHES

So how do you keep your poly-dates straight? When you're going on multiple dates with multiple people, you will eventually get confused about where you went with whom, what you wore on which date, who you told what, and which biographical data belongs to whom. It sounds very complicated—because it is!—but it is worth it for the greater good. Once again, it's time to break out the computer and power up Excel. On page 174 is an example of a spreadsheet I created when I was poly-dating to help me keep track of all these details.

I'm pretty sure all the guys on there would have been petrified had they found out about my spreadsheet, but I didn't know what else to do—there were too many details I needed to keep track of. Being that there are only seven days in a week, finding time to date multiple prospects in between having a full-time job, working out, and spending time with family and friends means you will be very busy! It will be hard to find time to spend with all the prospects each week, which means you will be scheduling lunch dates, dinner dates, coffee dates, drink dates, brunch dates, and any other types of date you can think of (and all that food means you will have to commit to getting to the gym!).

Eventually, things will get more serious with someone and you will have to break things off with the others. With most it will be easy just being honest: Tell them you've met someone and want to give it your full attention to see where it will go. With some, it may get messy, as they may have just had the same talk with their other prospects but with you in mind as that person they want to get more serious with. Those conversations will suck, but they are inevitable.

What I realized when I was poly-dating, and what you will soon realize yourself, is that one of the best things about dating more than one prospect at a time is that you don't allow yourself to fall for any one prospect too quickly. Admit it, this has probably happened to you. You like someone, you think the feelings are mutual, you get excited and start telling people you're dating someone, you start bringing your new prospect out with your friends, you make plans for the future, and, yes, you even think about how your names sound together . . . but then you get the rug pulled out from beneath you when you least expect it because you were mentally

Dates	Prospect 1	Prospect 2	Prospect 3	Prospect 4	Prospect 5
Name, Age, Profession	Isaac, 32, Website Developer	Jonah, 34, Contractor	Benjamin, 34, Small Biz Owner	Abraham, 32, Lawyer	Jacob, 33, Marketing
Family, Hometown, Schools	Parents divorced, 1 brother, from San Francisco, USC	Parents in Israel, 1 sister also in Israel, from Tel Aviv, no college	Parents married and living in Miami, 3 sisters and 1 brother, from New York, Columbia	Parents married, 2 sisters, from Los Angeles, UCLA	Single mom, only child, from Phoenix, ASU
How We Met	Mixer in January	Friend in January	JDate in February	JDate in February	Mixer in February

Dates	Prospect 1	Prospect 2	Prospect 3	Prospect 4	Prospect 5
1st Date: when, where, what I wore, other special info	February 28, Il Fornaio, navy blue silk dress, shared love of stupid movies	January 16, Marzipan, light pink lace top with jeans and tall brown boots, doesn't eat fish	March 2, Soleil, black tiered dress and tall black boots, major chemistry, amazing first kiss	February 22, La Trattoria, white silk top with jeans and black stilettos, could be a player	January 24, Sushi Sasa, navy silk dress, laughed a lot, not sure how I feel
2nd Date	March 6, The Market, cream dress, lots of hand-holding, really nice kiss	January 22, The Treehouse, black tiered dress, loves college fcootball and N=L	still making plans	March 1, picnic and a walk, still trying to figure him out but we have lots in common	keeps texting me but hasn't made an effort to make plans nor would I accept now
3rd, 4th and 5th Dates	still making plans	February 6, February 14th (Valentine's Day! brought me roses!), February 20		March 10, he's definitely poly-dating as well, good chemistry, we have fun	
Current Rank as of March 12	3	1	2	4	5

and emotionally more invested in the relationship than the other person was. But when you're busy dating other prospects—not sleeping around, just spending time together and getting to know them—you don't have time to think too much about one person.

On the flipside, dating multiple people at one time isn't always fun. Although it may increase your odds of finding your beshert, it can also hinder your chances at giving one person a fair shake. The previous chart shows five prospects narrowed down to two with a third still pending. Three is realistic, and six is too much because it's just too confusing. Dating two or three prospects or at least being open to casually dating more than one prospect is the whole point of this mind-set.

GET THE MOST OUT OF YOUR DATES

Maybe you've held on to your job during this economic downturn, maybe you've had to dip into your 401k, or maybe you've even had to move back in with your parents as you try to save money. It doesn't matter how the recession has affected you—if you're single and dating, then you're not going to stop going out no matter how hard your wallet's been hit. Whether you're dating for the fun of it or seriously looking for someone to share the rest of your life with, the types of dates you're now going out on may have to change because of the United States' financial mess.

In the long run, a JDate membership isn't expensive and is worth keeping. Think about how many drinks you'd have to buy at a bar in one month for yourself, your friends who you dragged out with you, and the prospects you're meeting. JDate is definitely cheaper than all that fuss. Instead, save your money for an actual date with a great prospect you meet on JDate.

Once you're on a date, you may have to cut corners. There are a few ways to save money without being too obvious about it. Besides, would you really want to date the type of person who is easily impressed by valet parking or a $400 tab? Trust me, your dates will be more impressed by the smooth ways you're being financially responsible, because chances are your date is going through something similar. Apart from finding free street parking (don't drive around in circles though, that's a big turnoff), you can also find really amazing hole-in-the-wall restaurants that won't break the bank. Do your research, ask your friends, and be imaginative. Do you really have to go to the hottest, newest restaurant when you can instead go to a quieter, tastier place? And when you're there, propose splitting an appetizer and the dessert—it's romantic and is cost conscientious in a subtle way.

You don't need to buy a new outfit for every date; instead use your closet—and those of your friends—wisely. Be aware that being taken out on a nice date in these times is an exception, not the rule, and therefore show your appreciation when this happens to you. Realize that if you don't go to the most expensive restaurant in town, your date may be trying to be fiscally responsible—a trait you should be looking for in a mate, recession or no recession.

There are so many things you can do on a date besides going to a restaurant, a bar, or the movies. Daytime dates can be just as romantic and tend to last longer than nighttime dates . . . and sometimes daytime dates can lead to nighttime dates. Packing a picnic for the beach or the mountains is sweet. If this is your third or fourth date, make it a night in and cook. If you wouldn't know what a cookbook looks like if it hit you in the head, then simply Google your date's favorite meal and follow the recipe step-by-step. There are also some perfectly romantic and cost-free activities you can take advantage of: Find an easy trail and take a hike at dusk, or stroll on the beach at sunset, or, if you discovered you both have a love for a certain sport, then grab that Frisbee or ball or what have you and engage in some friendly competition.

Since this recession doesn't seem to be ending anytime in the near future, we all need to make lifestyle changes. It's not going to be fun, but, in the end, you'll feel rewarded. Not only will you have accumulated funds in a savings account, but you'll also have landed a significant other who appreciates your responsible ways. It's a win-win.

♥ Julie

Julie was recently on a blind date with Darren. Darren is an NJB (nice Jewish boy) who just moved to town. He's a veterinarian, about six feet tall, and better-than-average looking. Plus he had the endorsement of the matchmaker, so Julie knew he must be a good guy and was eager to meet him. On their first date, Julie and Darren met for drinks and had a really great time. There was constant and natural conversation, there were plenty of commonalities, and there was mutual interest in seeing each other again, so it seemed as though Darren felt a connection as well.

Darren texted Julie the following Thursday morning, and she was savvy enough to respond in a way to get him to pick up the phone and call her rather than communicate via text. Once he called, they made plans to get dinner and catch a comedy show that Saturday night. Julie felt it was a bit late in the week to make Prime Time Date Night plans, but she liked the guy so she made an exception—which I wholeheartedly approved. Thursday morning is border-line for planning a weekend date, but there's no reason it shouldn't be accepted if you're available.

So for their second date, Darren picked Julie up from her place on Saturday night, where the plan was to walk to dinner and then the theater. As soon as they walked out the door, Darren asked Julie where she wanted to eat. Julie was taken aback by the fact that he didn't have any restaurant plans in mind—he did after all buy the comedy show tickets in advance, so she assumed he had put some thought into dinner as well—but she quickly rebounded and suggested a new Middle Eastern place nearby. Dinner conversation didn't flow quite as well as it did the week before, and, when the bill came, Julie made a move toward her wallet and offered her credit card, and Darren accepted. And as they were leaving the restaurant and entering and exiting the theater, Darren not only failed to hold the door open for Julie, but he let it fall shut behind him as he kept walking. Darren's lack of manners as well as his failure to make dinner reservations and his acceptance of Julie paying the bill was crushing Ju-lie, as she had been really excited about the prospect of Dar-ren but was looking for a man who was more chivalrous.

Darren went out of town for a week the morning after their date, and, during that time, I convinced Julie to give him another chance if he asked her out again. A few days after Darren returned from his trip, she received a text from him that said, "it was nice 2 meet u but I think we would b better off just as friends." Julie wasn't so crushed because of the last date letdown, but she was still perplexed. I reminded her of the multiple things he'd done during their last date that she hadn't appreciated and pointed out that at least he was nice enough to not leave her hanging. We'll never know what went wrong between date one and date two, nor why Darren wouldn't give it one more shot, but he probably had a list with a few of his own grievances against Julie, blunders she committed unknowingly.

So how does something so promising fail so quickly, and how can singles keep these little disappointments from getting the best of them? The emotional roller coaster is unfortunately a normal part of dating, and only hindsight will help you see that the roller coaster is weeding out the losers in the end. And by "losers" I simply mean those that are not right for you because they are perfect for someone else. It's better that the second date was such a doozy for both Julie and Darren because they didn't waste any more time on something that ultimately wasn't going to work out. Luckily, both of them saw the signs and neither was overly disappointed. Maybe it's realism, maybe it's pessimism, but rather than getting your hopes up super high for each new date, try to just get your hopes up, say, medium high with a dash of sensibility.

If you went on a first date that was a high but then the second date was a low, I'd give you the same advice I gave to Julie: Give it one more chance to see if the third date rebounds to a high, and then make the effort to keep it up there. After a certain point dating one person, you should be having few-to-no lows with little-to-no effort. Lows are a reality in a relationship, but, when you're still just dating, they shouldn't keep happening or happen all that often. Everyone's going to have their bad days, their foul moods. At the same time, if it's all highs, then it's probably not reality—no one is happy and perfect all the time even when they're on their best behavior for a date. If the first date is a low, then of course it's understandable to not want to give it a second chance, but what if it was a fluke? Use your instinct to tell you when it's not a match versus when you should be willing to give it another go.

♥ Natalie

Natalie's been implementing the poly-dating mind-set because she realized she was falling for guys way too easily and way too quickly. It seemed to be working until she wrote me with her current conundrum: She really likes two of the guys she's dating, and she can't decide which one to break it off with. She knows it may not be totally up to her, but she's pretty sure they both feel strongly toward her and she needs to make a move now before it becomes more difficult.

Luckily for Natalie (and unfortunately for me), I've been in this same situation, so I was able to lend Natalie advice based on my own experience. I had met two guys when I was in the midst of a poly-dating phase of my life. One guy worked with me, and I met the other guy at a mixer. I had been dating more than a few guys at the time but had slowly let the others go until I was down to these two, and then I was stuck. Surely these guys knew I was holding back, as I was still only seeing them each once or twice a week, and, although I was naturally flirtatious, I hadn't let the physical chemistry get the best of me.

My coworker was a great guy: He was ambitious and climbed the ranks at a young age, he was creative and always planned fun dates, and he was sweet, always remembering special dates. But he was also my coworker, and we weren't really supposed to be dating. If we did break up, it would be more awkward than going to management to let them know about our relationship. The guy from the mixer was also really great: He was an entrepreneur who was passionate about his business, he had a lot of great hobbies he liked to include me in, and most important he was active in the Jewish community. There was something a little off about him that I couldn't put my finger on, but there was also something really special about him that I couldn't ignore.

I ultimately chose the mixer guy. Things became awful at work because my now-ex wouldn't speak to me. I found out later he had been really into me and had already asked his supervisors about pursuing our relationship. But I had made the right decision for me, and things with the mixer guy got really serious once I let my guard down and truly became available. Of course, after a few months, the thing that felt off about him reared its ugly head in the form of an ex-girlfriend whom he still harbored feelings for. But because of those few months that the relationship was good, I knew I had made the right choice.

You have to recognize and trust a gut feeling. Neither guy ended up being right for me, but, at that time, one was more right than the other. If you're having trouble trusting your instincts, try and imagine yourself with each of the prospects down the road—can you picture having a conversation with each person in a month, a year, ten years?

Can you imagine yourself living with each person, marrying each person, parenting with each person? That may sound extreme, but, if you are dating someone with the hope that marriage is in your future, these are the tough questions you need to ask yourself. That said, keep this process and your poly-dating past to yourself. Prospects don't want to hear there are other potentials in your life even if they are also dating others, and they for sure don't want to know that you can't choose between them and another. Nor should you ever tell them you chose them over everyone else because the "everyone else" is the part that will stick out, not the "I choose you" part.

 ## Mike

Mike met another great girl, Kelly, on JDate last week, and for once he liked her enough that their first phone conversation lasted ninety minutes (Mike thinks this is great, but I know better and told him so later). Suddenly it was 11:00 PM, they were still chatting, and they realized they lived a block away from each other. He asked her if she would meet him at a bar on their street to continue the conversation. Kelly agreed, and downstairs they both went. That conversation ended up lasting another three hours until the bar was closing. He then asked her if she wanted to come up to his place but was pleased when she declined the invitation. When they started making plans to see each other again, they found out they wouldn't be able to meet up for nearly a month—Kelly was going back home for ten days to be with her family for the holidays, and before she got back Mike would be leaving for a two-week trip. So how does this pair keep up the momentum they so quickly gained when they won't be able to see each other for a month and won't even be able to talk on the phone for part of the time?

It was so great to finally hear Mike say he really liked a girl, that she was really cool, and he was really excited to see her again. So I was bummed to hear it would be a month before they could continue to develop their romance. So many things had to happen and, inversely, not happen, to aide them during the hiatus. First, and most important, neither of them could meet anyone else who tickled their fancy during that time. Mike was going to continue poly-dating, but Kelly had definitely taken the space at the top of the list. Second, and just as important, they had to keep in touch to a point: They needed to be sure to talk on the phone before Mike left for his trip and exchange a few emails while he was away. Thirdly, and conversely, they needed to be careful not to build up too much of a rapport while separated because then they could run the risk of creating unreachable expectations for one another. There's a fine line between keeping in touch, keeping the flame alive, and keeping the momentum going and starting a serious relationship via the phone and Internet before spending enough time together in person.

Having a month of phone calls and emails after meeting each other only once means you will only get the person on his or her best behavior. You also won't get to see facial expressions on the phone or hear vocal inflections in an email. That means when you see each other again in person, you may not know each other as well as you think you do. It's hard not to build someone up in your mind after a romantic night together, but as long as Mike and his new crush go into this month apart and into their reunion with realistic expectations, then I think they will do just fine picking up where they left off.

💜 Lauren

Lauren called me last night with a new dating debacle. After realizing she couldn't get past the Seth thing and broke up with him, she finally completed her JDate profile and almost instantly received an email from Yossi, whom she found to be intriguing. They went out, and the date went really well; there was chemistry and they had a lot in common (including many mutual friends), and they made plans to see each other again. After the date, the problem reared its ugly head. Lauren, not having dated or been in the singles scene for nearly fifteen years, didn't know who had a reputation in the singles circle. She knew Yossi had seriously dated one friend of hers and had gone out with a few others, and she didn't mind. But when she approached some other mutual friends to tell them about the great guy she went out with from the community named Yossi, her excitement took a nosedive at their reaction. All of these mutual friends had all dated Yossi as well! And she started to hear more and more rumors about additional friends and acquaintances who had also dated him. It turns out Yossi is an over-the-top poly-dater who doesn't understand the meaning of discretion.

Yossi is actively looking for his beshert and is willing to turn over every rock until he finds her. He really wants to get married and has dated every relatively attractive woman in the area. With some women it only lasted one or two dates, and with others he had long-term relationships. None of the women had anything bad to say about Yossi, just that "it" wasn't there. When Yossi runs into his exes at mixers or on the street, they greet him cordially with a warm hug. There is no animosity. But there's also no concrete reason any of them stopped dating. There's just something they can't quite put their fingers on.

Instinctually, I didn't think Yossi was right for Lauren, but I thought he would be good dating practice, so I explained my thought process to her and softened the edges about what poly-dating is. I told her she shouldn't have a problem with someone who has dated everyone possible; it just means they are looking for the same thing as her. As long as her friends who dated the guy give her their blessing and warn her if there's anything worth knowing, I say he's free game. Lauren had realistic reasons to be concerned, but she had already been on a date with him and enjoyed herself, so why should she restrict herself just because other people's dates with him didn't go as well? Had she not gone and asked each friend about him, she would only have known about the few mutual friends and not the expanded list, and she would have gone on a second date with him without any pretense or preconceived notions. I told her I would be more concerned if she didn't know one person whom he had dated. Yossi was obviously committed to finding a Jewish woman, and that's exactly the type of guy Lauren was looking for.

Given the opportunity, I would tell Yossi not to play Jewish Geography until at least a third date and rather to spend the time concentrating on the woman he's with. Sure, it's important to eventually get endorsements from your mutual friends, but, when you've dated all of those friends, the endorsement isn't quite as meaningful and could end up hurting you more than helping you. Better to allow your date to form his or her own opinion first.

Beth

Beth has a huge wall up. She's been hurt and disappointed so much that she's lost the zest for dating. There's an acceptable wall, and then there's Beth's wall, which is made out of brick covered by concrete covered by wood that's been nailed and glued solid. Beth has stopped letting anyone in but still wonders why women don't want a second date. Her wall is built thick and solid, and it will take a lot of patience by a woman to saw, chisel, and finally knock it down. Beth thinks she is protecting herself, but, in actuality, she's hurting herself. By not letting anyone in, she won't get hurt because she won't be getting asked out on very many second dates or have very many second date proposals accepted. What's even worse is that when I ask her why she's so guarded, she says she isn't. Whether she's in denial or whether the wall truly is subconscious, it's detrimental to her love life. You can't and won't fall in love if you don't let anyone in. Beth is going to lengthen her single life until she realizes she needs to open up more. The way I see it, a wall is only there for someone to break down—but it would be a heck of a lot easier if the person with the wall could acknowledge the wall's existence to begin with!

Chances are, the people with such a wall up were hurt badly in the past and are scared. I get that. It's the reason many singles keep to the same script on first dates. They only want to let the person get to know them a certain, pre-measured amount, and they want to control that amount because they've been on one of those first dates where they talked for hours and hours only to never see the other person again. Why bother exchanging anything more than pleasantries until you know if there could be another date? You don't want to become invested until you know if there will be a return. This is the normal, human type of wall that most people, not just singles, seem to have naturally put up to protect themselves.

 ## David

David is poly-dating without trying because he's going out with various women, but he doesn't have time for a spread-sheet nor does he need one, since he doesn't end up dating these women for very long. David is continuously going on dates, and he has usually been able to tell after the first or second date if the woman is worth his time, so his poly-dating gets narrowed down quickly and often. At the very most, David will overlap two women at a time, but, once a woman gets past the second date and they plan a third date, David won't consider dating any other women.

This is smart for someone like David who is new to the dating scene after a long time and is attracting more women than he knows what to do with. David narrows down prospects before even asking a woman out on a first date and then is very instinctual when it comes to who he wants to see again. David, like Beth, has a wall up, but for very different reasons. He automatically compares women to his late wife, and, although he knows no one will measure up to her and that he doesn't want the exact same type of woman as her, he can't help but eliminate prospects that way. But David at least has an actual person to which he's comparing women, rather than some convoluted, ever-changing vision in his head like most singles compare their prospects to. Although David's version of poly-dating isn't exactly being implemented the way I advise, it's the thought that counts. His mind-set is the important part here; he's being open to having two of the women he's dating overlap until one gets more serious or gets eliminated.

Chapter 10

✦ GETTING SERIOUS ➤

AFTER GOING ON MANY dates and eliminating each poly-date prospect until you are down to one, it's time for The Talk. You're at a point where you have to have a hopefully pressure-free and mutual, lovey-dovey chat about not seeing other people, about being committed to each other, and about taking the relationship to the next level. Being monogamous is an exciting step that will bring lots of discoveries with it: Spending more time together means spending less time with your friends. Spending more time together means more opportunities to get into arguments. Spending more time together means more time to have embarrassing things happen to you in front of your new boyfriend or girlfriend. Spending more time together can lead you to realize you don't want to be with that person anymore, or it can lead you to realize you've met the person you could spend the rest of your life with. By getting serious with someone, you are also taking the chance at getting your heart broken. Alas, this is a risk you must take.

COUPLED UP AND SINGLED OUT

If you look around a mixer, a wedding, or any other party, you'll notice the singles and the couples are almost always segregated. It's not that the two groups dislike each other, but it seems they can no longer relate to one another. Couples act like their memory of single life was completely wiped away when they found their beshert. Are they trying to forget how much fun being single was or how unbearably depressing it can get? Are they remembering the excitement of meeting someone new or the loneliness of seeing the same faces over and over again? Singles have a hard time understanding the desire to go home from a party on the early side of midnight, whereas couples don't generally want to stay up until dawn drinking, dancing, and flirting. Couples often act like singles have the plague, while singles often yearn to meet someone so badly they have no interest in interacting with other couples.

The problem with couples is the way they can become cliquey once they partner up. They often act like having a significant other means they've joined an exclusive club that singles are not allowed in to. Back in my midtwenties dating heyday, some of my coupled friends decided to take pity on me and invited me to game night. The rest of the invitees included four other couples and my good friend Sarah. Sarah is one of my best friends, but she and I are not a couple, and inviting us to a couple's game night together because we were the hosts' two single friends was insulting. I don't think the hosts were being malicious or trying to offend Sarah or me, but I was offended nonetheless.

My married friends loved living vicariously through my dating stories, and I know I should have been flattered, but, honestly, I'd have been more than happy to change places with any of them (no one ever offered) if it meant never again getting hit on by guys at

Jewish events who were old enough to be my dad (some were in fact my friends' fathers).

I don't understand why a new phase in life means forgetting about the people who were there for you before. It's understandable that friendships will change, but to completely dismiss them is incomprehensible. On the one hand, you should accept being single—and suffer through couple's game nights—for as long as it takes to meet your beshert. You should refuse to settle and possibly become another statistic in the heightened divorce rate (take it from me!). When you do become part of a couple, don't forget what it was like to be out there dating, and don't act like your single friends have a sickness or that you're better than them because you don't have to be out there dating anymore.

Now that you have the boyfriend/girlfriend title, don't let it go to your head. Your friends were there for you throughout this journey, so, now that you have a significant other, don't forget about them. It's always the same tune, different song: When you're single and looking, you usually surround yourself with your single friends for going out and your coupled-up friends for hanging out. Then once you start dating someone and it gets serious, you almost always drop contact with most (if not all) of your friends and become completely immersed in the new relationship. Your single friends are often put by the wayside, and, normally, only once your relationship reaches the level of double-dating, do you commence communicating with your coupled-up friends. In most situations, your single friends only resurface once they are no longer single or after you become single again.

It's natural to want to hang out with other couples when you become one of them, but it's sad when you lose sight of your devoted friends during a new phase in your life. It's understandable why it happens: When you're on the inside of something new, you want to spend all of your free time together, and, when you can't be together, you're on the phone or texting or emailing because it's new and exciting and you're getting to know each other better and falling in love. And even if you do pay some attention to your friends, your mind wanders back to your new relationship and you don't focus well on listening to what they have to say. Or all you do is talk about your new relationship until your friends lose their minds.

When you're the single friend being left out to dry, you hate it, yet you'll probably do the same thing when it's your turn. Every single needs to make a promise not to forget about his or her friends (or bore them to death with every last detail of your new relationship) when he or she becomes somebody's boyfriend or girlfriend. You will need and want your friends one day—whether this relationship makes it or not—so show them how much you appreciate them by not ditching them the minute you find love.

Your single friends will want to be spending time going to mixers and going out with other singles to bars and going on poly-dates, while couples are either out together, home together, on double dates with other couples, enjoying a girls' or guys' night out, or even indulging in a night alone. But just because your lives are not on the same paths at this moment doesn't mean you shouldn't work at maintaining a strong friendship.

It's natural to want to like being around couples once you're in a relationship and to not want to go anywhere near the single life you worked so hard to get away from. You paid your dues: You went to all the mixers, had a perfectly edited JDate profile, welcomed setups, and spent plenty of time commiserating about the dating scene with other singles. You're forgiven for not wanting anything to do with being single for a while and for wanting to just enjoy being part of a couple. That said, you're not part of a couple just to not be single anymore—you're coupled up because you really like this person!—and your single friends can help you keep that in perspective.

Hanging out with other couples is good for your relationship, too. Going on double dates and getting together as a group of couples will help you feel more like a couple. You get to share stories about the perils of living together, fighting, planning for the future, and other day-to-day doldrums. And being alone with your friends who are also in relationships can be considered a type of couples therapy. You can bitch and moan about your significant other without being afraid of seeming insensitive to your single friends who would give anything to be in a relationship right now. And you can talk about how great the partners in your lives are with your coupled friends, whereas it would be like bragging in front of your single friends. It's a lose-lose situation to either complain or boast in front of your single friends.

I hated when my newly coupled friends spent less time with me, but now I understand. It wasn't that they were snobs; it was that they didn't want to be reminded of the single life and they simply had less in common with me because I was still single. But if you're in a new relationship, try to make a conscious effort to remember how fed up with being single you felt at times, so when your single friends need to complain, you can empathize. You don't want to be one of those people who becomes so absorbed with being in a relationship that you can't have a conversation anymore without saying "my boyfriend this" or "my girlfriend that." Keep your boasting or complaining about your new relationship to your coupled-up friends, and make a conscious effort to be a good friend to your still-single friends when they need to bitch and moan about dating.

GETTING INTO FIGHTS

The longer you're with someone and the more time you spend together, the more opportunity there is to get into arguments. You might be in a pissy mood and your significant other is doing things he or she normally does, but, this time, the gum-snapping or finger-tapping or loud chewing is irking you to no end, and it causes you to lose your temper and make a snide comment, which in turn becomes a full-blown argument about nothing. Or something very important in one of your lives might occur, you find that you adamantly disagree with how your significant other dealt with the occurrence, which causes a rift.

I hear so many singles say and believe that "love shouldn't take work." My response to that statement is this: "You need to work to find love, and once you find it you must continue to work to maintain it, and, on top of that, is it worth it if you don't have to work for it?" The type of work you put into a relationship determines whether it is the type of love that is worth it. If you spend more time fighting and making up than you do getting along, then you need to determine if the work it takes when things are bad is worth the times when things are good. Everyone fights, but what is the healthy ratio of getting along to fighting that makes the work valuable? And how soon is too soon to start fighting? What level of fighting is healthy, and when does it go too far? These are important questions to ask yourself when dating someone turns into a more serious relationship and you realize the reality is that you may not always get along.

There's no rulebook when it comes to fighting when you're dating, but you must remind yourself and your significant other that respect needs to be the foundation of your relationship. Alas, at some point, the gloves will come off and the fangs will come out.

You both might say things you don't mean, and you both might say things to deliberately hurt your loved one, and you both might say things you can't take back. Fighting is an art when you're in a relationship because often you're in the heat of the moment and aren't thinking straight, and thus words come out of your mouth before you can edit them. Add Jewish guilt to the mix, and suddenly the war of the words can become a cry-fest, the blameworthy twisting words to turn him or herself into the victim.

The thing about fighting while you're in a relationship is you have to decide if it's worth it. If the relationship is new and you're already fighting, then you may need to take a step back and look at it from a new perspective. Are you both people who are passionate and enjoy arguing and, of course, the intimate making up? Or are you just not a match and need to break up and move on? Speaking of breaking up, if you're bouncing in and out of the same relationship, you may be addicted to drama. It's hard to see a bad relationship when you're the one in it, and it's even harder to be told you're in one from an outside source. If a number of your loved ones have either tried talking to you about your relationship or have distanced themselves from you, take the hint. Don't be stuck having to use the excuse that "hindsight is 20/20" because you didn't follow your instincts.

As a relationship matures, it's normal to argue, fight, yell, and even enforce the silent treatment every once in a while. Calling each other nasty names is not normal, threatening to end the relationship during every tiff is not normal, and hitting is definitely not normal. Those types of threats are absolutely unacceptable. If someone is violent toward you, end the relationship immediately.

The other thing that's not normal is never, ever disagreeing. If you never have an argument, that doesn't mean your relationship is perfect, it means you're not being honest with yourself or each other. It means there are probably bigger, weightier issues lying below the surface, and those types of problems will eventually erupt.

Just because a couple fights doesn't mean they can't have a successful marriage . . . as long as they both agree divorce isn't an option. Once you say the *sheva brachot* under the chuppah and exchange those solid bands symbolizing eternity, any fighting must be resolved because you can't break up as easily as you did when you were single. Nobody wants to become like Ross Geller, the Jewish guy from *Friends*, and be divorced three times by the time they're in their thirties. At the same time, you can enter into a marriage with the best of intentions and still end up having to get a get. Not every marriage is destined for success, but thankfully for the Chosen People, the divorce rate among innerfaith Jewish relationships is lower than the national average.

When you are fighting, make sure you listen to your partner: Let your partner speak his or her piece, respect his or her opinion, and then relay your side. You won't resolve anything unless you hear each other out. Compromise is a must, and it doesn't matter who's right or who's wrong. But if you are wrong, own up to it and apologize. But don't just use the word "sorry" as a way to avoid arguments because you think that's what your partner wants to hear. Trust me, I'm right about this. Unfortunately, not everyone fights healthily or productively, which makes making up after a fight more difficult the more often it happens.

It's common for two people with strong personalities to be attracted to each other, and therefore it shouldn't be surprising when their relationship is a volatile one. Some people thrive off volatility (think of the Hollywood couples who grace the tabloid covers regularly), but, for most of us, it does not make for a healthy relationship. If you spend too much time fixing your relationship and not enough time actually being in and enjoying your relationship, then you need to end that relationship and move on.

RED FLAGS

If there's drama early on in your relationship, it may be a red flag. Purposefully making your significant other jealous, going into rages over seemingly unimportant issues, and constantly getting into fights with family and friends can all be red flags. If you don't agree about what is drama or how to deal with it, it may also be a red flag. And these are not red flags to ignore. You need to be aware of these red flags so you don't consciously or subconsciously overlook them because you're hoping for the relationship to work. It doesn't mean the relationship is necessarily doomed, but it does mean you need to have a talk. People who are drama magnets and thrive off it probably won't mesh well with people who avoid it and don't like to fan the flames.

People who create drama or put themselves in the midst of drama usually do so because they're either bored, immature, or both. Hopefully, a healthy and exciting romantic relationship will be enough to quell the urge for hullabaloo. Eventually, sitting at home with your significant other watching television on the couch while cuddling will be much more enjoyable and productive than spending your time on the phone instigating drama, arguing about nonsense, or ignoring your mate.

Once you learn how to fight productively and with respect, you will find that many other areas of your relationship will thrive as well. A few tips for fighting healthy include:

- Don't try to talk it out in the heat of the moment. Take a breather and give each other some space, and then reconvene to discuss the matter calmly.

- Sit down, hold hands, and maintain eye contact to help lower the tension and connect back to each other.

- Don't bring up the past or go for the jugular; fight fair.

- Remind yourself who you're fighting with and what you're fighting about, and then ask yourself if it's worth it.

EMBARRASSING MOMENTS

The more time you spend with someone, the more chance there is that you will do something embarrassing. At the beginning of a relationship, totally normal things that will eventually become commonplace once you're living together will cause you to want to crawl under a rock and cower as you blush deep colors of crimson.

Sorry guys, but it's true: Girls pass gas, burp, and use the bathroom just like every other human being. I know there's a rumor going around that women are immune to those natural occurrences, but it ain't so. Women may be able to hide those bodily functions better than you, but they still happen. And the longer you hang out with a lady, the harder it gets for her to hide those occurrences.

Being in a relationship means spending a lot of time with another person: days, weekends, and, hopefully, eventually, forever. That much time together means there is going to be ample opportunity for your natural bodily functions to rear their ugly heads in both noisy and smelly ways. And there's absolutely nothing you can do about it. You drink some soda, you're forced to burp. You eat beans, you're forced to fart. You eat too much too fast, you're forced to belch. Holding back any of these gasses will only make you uncomfortable and bloated. Letting these gasses out will only make you feel uncomfortable and bewildered.

There are some tried and true techniques you can use to do what you gotta do without it being heard, seen, or sniffed. It means you have to use your time and opportunities wisely. Excuse yourself to go to the restroom and turn on both the fan and the faucet to stifle any sounds. Use the public restrooms at the movie theater or at a restaurant instead of the one in the apartment that doesn't have any ventilation and has a toilet that tends to clog. Excuse yourself to go outside to make a "phone call" and pass wind in the wind. You can also carry around a few helpful items in your overnight bag: antacids, Gas-X, deodorant, mouthwash, and face wipes always come in handy.

It's when you feel comfortable doing those things in front of your new guy or gal that you know you're in a strong relationship. There will be very few people with whom you will get to that point, and it can be the agent to introduce an awkward conversation once somebody finally drops the (stink) bomb. On the bright side, this talk may force your relationship to the next level. Unfortunately, this talk may only lead to further exposure of all your disgusting habits.

Some people use their burps and farts as a dating technique. They figure if a guy or gal can withstand their noises and smells, then they're a keeper. If they're grossed out, then it wasn't meant to be. Interestingly enough, most people I know who use this technique do not find that their partner has a problem with their, well, problem. It's a risky move though, and not one I suggest to use freely.

If you don't think your new boy- or girlfriend is ready to handle you in all your natural glory, then maybe you should hold off for now on introducing him or her to all the different "noises" you're capable of. It's when your significant other thinks your farts and burps are cute that you may have found yourself a keeper. Just don't overdo it—nobody likes to be smoked out of his or her own bed because a lactose intolerant lover decided to eat pizza and ice cream even though he or she didn't have a Lactaid pill to take first.

GETTING COZY

Now that you're in a committed, monogamous relationship, you will also have ample opportunity to get cozy, cuddle up, and spend the night. Not all cuddlers are created equal, and most people are not used to sharing their beds, so it can take some adjustment.

"Are you a cuddler?" should be added to JDate's questionnaire because knowing if someone cuddles is just as important as knowing if someone smokes or drinks or likes dogs. Cuddlers and noncuddlers just don't mix. You either like being touchy-feely, kissy-huggy, or you don't, but if you were able to make the cuddling question a prerequisite, there wouldn't be any problem. Matching a cuddler and a noncuddler will only make for a lot of frustration, although it is not totally hopeless as long as they're willing to meet in the middle—somewhere between hand-holding and stuffing their hands into each other's back pockets.

Some people need the hand-holding, hugging, having an arm around them, finding that spot in the nook of the shoulder where their head fits, folding themselves into their partner for a little spooning, and so on, to make them feel protected and loved. Others are content with grabbing your hand every now and then for a few seconds or laying a hand on your thigh while driving and watching a movie, but they draw the line at massaging feet, nibbling at ears, or cuddling while sleeping.

One friend of mine had to break up with a girl who refused to cuddle. She wouldn't compromise, and he wasn't willing to be in a relationship without physical affection. On the flipside, another friend of mine isn't a big cuddler, and, when she was thinking about breaking up with her boyfriend, she had to take into consideration the fact that he wouldn't stop touching her even after she told him it made her uncomfortable. Some people can make it work, and some can't. At the end of day, it depends on how much you like the other person and how much you're willing to compromise.

There are many degrees of cuddling, but, when it comes to public displays of affection, or PDA, there are just two sides. Either you're okay with a few kisses here and there, or you are willing to engage in a full-on make-out session. As much as most of us love witnessing love, being a part of love, or helping to create love, the vast majority of people do not want to watch tonsil hockey, spit-swapping, or sucking face while eating, drinking, walking through the park, or watching a movie.

PDA is like a car accident: It's disturbing, but you can't help but stare. At the beginning of falling in love, you can't keep your hands off each other, and you want everyone to know you're in love. Alas, you don't need to broadcast your love in a distasteful manner—when you're really in love it will show in your eyes, on your face, and in your subtle touches and kisses. The people who can't keep their hands off each other aren't anymore in love than other couples who don't engage in PDA.

Sleeping in a bed with someone for the first time is always an interesting experience. By sleeping, I'm referring to getting some shuteye, resting, snoozing, napping, catching some z's . . . I'm not talking about sex. That will be covered in Chapter 11, Kosher Sex. The first night you share a bed with your new partner, you won't want to move, make noises, or do those awkward and embarrassing things we do on a normal night in bed alone. When you first begin spending the night, it will likely take an inordinate amount of time for you to fall asleep. You will try to lie there still as a log, doing steady yoga breathing, all the while making sure you look cute (clothes placed properly and as many fresh-breath items nearby as possible). Eventually you will fall asleep and guess what? Your body will shift positions and your clothes will fall into disarray and morning breath will creep up and you may even let a fart fly.

Pillow talk is something you begin engaging in during the beginning stages of your romance. You'll lay there until far too late into the night having deep conversations and opening up to each other in ways you weren't comfortable doing so with the light on. Some people can fall asleep the second their heads hit the pillow, while others like to chat away until sleep catches up with them.

Then there's picking a side of the bed. The resident may have a preference, but, if not, you have to think about where you subconsciously end up sleeping when alone. Never thought you'd have to think about these things, did you? Not everyone stays on their side of the bed of course; there are rollers, kickers, blanket-stealers, heat-seekers, and the all-too-typical one-leg-over-the-cover-to-keep-your-body-temperature-even sleepers.

As nice as cuddling sounds, you can't fall asleep when the blood flow leaves your arm because it's wedged under your significant other's torso. Nor can you fall asleep breathing in hot air because your face is smashed against your partner's chest or wedged into his or her underarm. And even though you try so hard to fall asleep together, you will almost always wake up on opposite sides of the bed. Sleeping—just sleeping—together is a very intimate part of a relationship.

SPENDING TOO MUCH TIME TOGETHER

When you're in the midst of the beginning stages of a relationship, you end up spending more time than normal together. Spending a lot of time together has its plusses and minuses. On one hand, you get to know each other really well, really quickly, and because of that the relationship can easily become really serious. Or you could get to know each other really well, really quickly, and because of that the relationship could easily end really badly.

When you're in the first phase of a relationship and all you want to do is hold hands, eat meals together, meet each other's friends, talk all the time, and simply not want to be apart, the time you would normally be on your best behavior falls victim to your true self and your worst habits. Again, this can either be a great thing or a catastrophe. The relationship could escalate, or it could head down disaster lane. Spending so much time together can often cause people to start getting on each other's last nerves and annoying each other to no end, and people might start finding fault in their partners where there is none.

Spending too much time together also means taking away the mystery and not getting the chance to miss each other. It's not about playing games; it's about letting your partner have a chance to think about you without you there. When you're next to each other 24/7, you may take your new partner for granted and even get sick of him or her when you should be fantasizing about your next date. If you can't remember what your best friends look like, you're spending too much time together with your new love. A regular "No-Girls-Allowed Poker Night" or "Girls Night Out" is healthy, fun, and, ironically, even more necessary than when you were single.

Unfortunately, if spending too much time together is causing the demise of a promising relationship, it's probably too late to resuscitate. But if you notice the issue early enough, then take measures immediately even if they seem drastic. First, talk about the problem, and rest assured the relationship will strengthen as you tackle this predicament together. Make plans apart so you can look forward to spending time together. Absence makes the heart grow fonder, right?

Seeing each other a few times a week, keeping in contact throughout the day (texting is acceptable at this point), and making sure you see your family and friends during the week as well will ensure you are spending a healthy amount of time together while also still taking your time adjusting into this phase of your relationship.

 Julie

Julie hasn't been in a serious relationship since college. There just isn't anyone whom she's met that she's been willing to let her guard down with, but there have been more than a dozen really high-quality guys who have come her way. Julie is sabotaging her own dating life by always finding something wrong with each guy. Some of the excuses may have been acceptable, but some were totally unfounded. One guy was eliminated because he owned cats and she is a dog person. (Simplifying that story sounds harsh—the guy had three cats and kept the litter box in his bedroom.) Another guy was let go after he confronted her when he saw that she had logged into JDate. Either he was a hypocrite because he was also still on JDate, or he was a stalker. Yet another guy got the boot because it took eight years and three universities for him to graduate with his bachelor's degree.

Luckily Julie is poly-dating right now, and there are some guys with great potential who she has yet to find any major faults with. I have a good feeling about these guys because of how Julie is talking about them and because of her positive attitude and excitement about dating (finally!), so I think The Talk is in her near future.

 Natalie

Natalie did finally end up choosing one of her poly-dates to move forward with. In fact, he made it difficult for her not to dump the other guy. His name is Ben, and he had also been out a lot, had been dating a lot, and had been having fun, but he was doing so with the idea of settling down in the back of his mind as soon as he found the right girl. As soon as Ben caught sight of Natalie, it was the end of him. It was a shocker they had never met because they had many mutual friends (who never thought to set them up for some reason). He knew she was his beshert, but he just had to convince her, which may have been a bit of a challenge since Natalie had been hurt by her ex-husband at a young age and was out partying to fill the void.

Once Ben knew Natalie was the one, the persistent romancing began. You see, Ben had recently found a website that customizes and sends greeting cards, so he began slyly getting to know Natalie through their dates and mutual friends and sending her card after card after card in between dates and before dates and after dates. Some included a funny photo of him with an even funnier caption. They ranged from: "Can I borrow a quarter? I want to call my mom and tell her I just met the girl of my dreams," to: "I looked up the word beautiful in the dictionary and there was a picture of you." The lines got cheesier and cheesier, but they made Natalie laugh.

Some cards had photographs of beautiful scenery, such as the beaches of Fiji, Tel Aviv, Greece, and Hawaii, accompanied by captions saying things like, "I hope to visit these places with you one day." Others were actual photos of Natalie that Ben had somehow pilfered from friends, and they included cute captions, such as, "You look hot here, but you'd look even better with me next to you." A few times he even Photoshopped the two of them into a cartoon drawing together. None of the cards asked her to get more serious than she was ready for, and, in fact, none of them put any pressure on her at all. He just kept sending greeting cards, and sometimes they even arrived with a box of brownies or candy or a puzzle.

Natalie wasn't creeped out by any of this, though others may have seen it as inappropriate obsession or infatuation. She thought it was sweet and cute, she enjoyed receiving the cards at random times, and she kept them all. And then one day, Ben sent her a card with a dozen red roses. It asked her to meet him on the beach at sunset. And so she went, already ready to have The Talk with him, and she brought with her all thirty-five cards he had sent her. When Ben handed her the

  HOW TO WOO A JEW

thirty-sixth card in person it asked her to "be his girlfriend," and, although it was cheesy, Natalie was charmed and said yes.

Ben felt that Natalie was somewhat out of his league, and so he went above and beyond what he had ever done before to attract a woman. He could tell she was someone special and was willing to pull out all the stops, take the time, and make the effort to appeal to her in a way she had probably never been romanced before. Natalie had been wined and dined by many a man, but she had never been made to feel as amazing as Ben made her feel—and she wanted to feel that way every day for the rest of her life and in return make him feel special, too.

Ben's effort is a great lesson in taking the extra step. People are so tired of being single that they no longer try hard. Instead of going through the normal doldrums of dating, try to spice it up by making a little more effort. Maybe Ben's tactic was a bit extreme, but I'm sure you can find something to make your date feel like he or she stands apart from the pack and hope that they do the same for you.

 ## Mike

Mike decided to take a risk and have The Talk with Kelly, one of the women he's been poly-dating for the past few months, the one with whom he shared an awesome first date before they both went out of town. His decision partly had to do with Kelly being great on paper (Jewish, smart, close to his age, attractive), partly to do with Mike feeling a need to take that step with someone, and partly because he has feelings for her (for all the reasons she's great on paper and more).

When Mike and Kelly met that first night, they both felt an instant attraction, and before too long there was physical intimacy between them. A few months after having The Talk, though the physical intimacy remains, their emotional connection has waned. Mike says his feelings for his girlfriend (a big word for Mike to use!) are strong, but he knows he should find someone better suited for him and is afraid he is staying with her because he feels obligated. His heart is telling him one thing while his head is telling him another—a common scenario. He asks, "Is anyone better than no one?"

At some point in your dating lifetime you will probably find yourself dating someone simply for the sake of not being alone. Better to spend your time with someone you don't like than spend another Saturday night at home alone, right? Wrong. If you're busy devoting time to someone you know isn't right for you, that's time taken away from the opportunity to meet someone who could be your beshert. You're cheating yourself and the other person. The longer you wait to end the relationship, the harder it will get. It's simply not a fair shake for either of you.

At some point in your dating lifetime you will probably find yourself dating someone, hoping that the feelings will grow and deepen as time goes on, and then you will suddenly realize that you're in the midst of a long-term relationship and that you don't quite know how you got there. Staying in a relationship with the anticipation of something developing is nice . . . in theory. You're giving the other person a chance, but you need be honest with yourself—if you're not feeling the other person after just a few months, then it's probably not going to work.

The overarching problem is that breaking it off is easier said than done, especially for Mike, who is completely aware of his situation and yet hasn't taken action to change it. The reason? Our hearts can often veto our heads. If you find yourself in any of the situations above, try making a Pros versus Cons list so you can see your dating life on paper. Sometimes seeing it in black and white is all it takes to get your head and your heart on the same page. I'm proud of Mike for taking a chance and giving the relationship a fair shake. It is more than he has done in years, and, although she may not be the right girl for him, he knows that he can at least find a great Jewish girl and make a commitment to her.

Lauren

Lauren went on one more date with Yossi before telling him she was looking for something different. She has been poly-dating slowly, as she has limited time as a single mom, and she has now been able to narrow down what she wants even more so than before. She gave a few guys who didn't have kids a chance, but there was something missing for her that only another parent could bring to the table. She tightened the radius on the miles away from her zip code a potential match could live because she realized she would never move her kids from their schools and that she did not have the time to travel more than thirty minutes for a date. One guy tried the belching and farting tactic with her, and it didn't go over well. Lauren was married ten years and has small children, so she is used to hearing and smelling bodily functions and is looking forward to dating like an adult.

Lauren is becoming more active on JDate and in the community, and she is finding there to be no shortage of positive male attention sent her way. One guy tried to have The Talk with her already, but she realized she is nowhere close to being ready for that, regardless of how amazing the guy is, and she is still happily poly-dating for now.

Beth

Beth may just very well be in love. She expanded the mileage that she was willing to search for potentials on JDate, she changed her profile to say "Willing to Relocate," and she met Andrea almost right away. Beth lives in Chicago, and Andrea lives in her small hometown in Wisconsin and isn't willing to move very far. So Beth is pondering the idea of leaving the big city—and her art world—for Andrea's small town, but she doesn't want the relationship to go any further until she knows how she feels.

Here's where it gets even more interesting: Beth actually found out about a great job as an Art History professor in Milwaukee, only a half-hour drive away from Andrea's town. If she takes the job, Beth can move closer to Andrea without moving "for" her and without moving into her small hometown where there's not even so much as an art gallery. If she can get this job—she's qualified for it and has been interested in a career move like this for a while—then she can move to Milwaukee, get her own place, and drive out to visit Andrea or clear her calendar on the weekends when she comes to visit her. Not only will Andrea not feel the pressure of Beth moving "for" her, but she also won't feel like Beth's giving up every-thing to be with her either. And hopefully Andrea will be moti-vated by Beth's big move to take the steps herself to leave the nest. If the relationship doesn't work out, then at least Beth's got her great new job in a city and isn't stuck in Andrea's small town (and still isn't all that far from Chicago either).

Making such a sacrifice is a big step for a person to take in a relationship. That person is the one laying everything on the line, including their pride. If the relationship didn't work out, then Beth would be the one feeling more dejected than Andrea because Andrea didn't have to sacrifice anything. Beth has decided she needs to do absolutely everything possible, including making sacrifices, to get what she wants, which is a partner in life. She comforts herself with the fact that Andrea had, after all, taken some risk in asking her to move to Wisconsin to begin with.

Pride often gets in the way of a relationship, and it's the first thing you have to be okay letting go of when you're in a complicated situation and want the relationship to succeed. Sometimes it may be something small, such as selling some of your items when you move in together or going to a sushi restaurant when you hate raw fish or making the first phone call after a fight. Sometimes it's big-ger, such as moving for the other person or letting go of friends who aren't supportive or accepting of your partner for whatever reason. The key here is that both parties need to sacrifice something or else run the risk of resentment ruining the relationship.

♥ David

David kept going out on dates with the same woman until everyone else fell by the wayside. They never had to have The Talk; everything just moved into place naturally. Karen is in her fifties, which means she is closer to David's age than his daughters'—something that was important to David. Karen is divorced with two older kids, so, although she can't empathize with losing a spouse, she does understand suddenly being single in the middle of your life after a long time and with grown children.

Karen is active and looks great for her age. She had tried JDate and was attending a monthly Jewish mixer for middle-aged singles, but mainly she was meeting new friends from those mediums, since she cut out and lost many friends during her divorce. David's daughters like Karen, and Karen's kids like David. On one hand they want to take it slow, but, on the other hand, they're adults and they know what they want and they don't have much time to waste. Since neither of them has any kids living with them at home, they get to spend the night with each other and have already created a strong bond based on an emotional, mental, and physical connection.

Neither David nor Karen ever thought they would have to date again, but they both have already done some soul-searching to make sure they're not settling with each other just because they don't want to be in the dating scene, and, so far, both of them have passed each other's respective intuition tests.

....

Chapter 11

 KOSHER SEX

THIS IS NOT THE CHAPTER where I lecture you about not having sex until marriage because, let's face it, short a few exceptions, almost everyone reading this book has already had sex, is having sex, and will continue to have sex (hopefully!). This is also not the chapter where I lecture you about using protection because, if you're not using it, you already know you should be. Condoms are cool. This chapter is about reading the signs that will help you decide when to have sex while dating and determine if it is going to hinder your romantic endeavors or help them. Each and every situation you are confronted with is going to be different: Sometimes giving it up is going to be the right choice and will move your relationship forward, and sometimes it will kill whatever it was that would probably have died eventually anyway.

SEX SIGNALS: TIMING
The basic theory most relationship experts agree upon regarding sex is this: If you want the relationship to get serious, then don't have

sex for a while. I'm not talking three dates here; I'm talking after a month of seeing each other multiple times a week. If you were actively poly-dating and are just now eliminating everyone else for this prospect, then after The Talk may be the right time. If you know this person has had a reputation in the past, then you may want to wait even longer until you've made it clear that you are different and that this relationship is different. If you know this specific prospect isn't your beshert but there's an intense sexual chemistry between you, then go ahead and have fun—just make sure the intentions are clear and the feelings (or lack thereof) are mutual.

If you are unsure how you feel about this person or you are unsure if you want to go all the way, then don't. Nothing good will ever come of having sex with someone when you're not ready. Conversely, there are plenty of couples who had sex on their first date and later got married. In discussing this chapter with friends and colleagues, I ended up having to sit through many stories like that from the middle-aged parents of my friends who had sex almost right away and are still happily married thirty-five years later. Can you say awkward? It was very sweet seeing these people still so very much in love after doing something so risky so long ago. The thing is, this is not the norm, at least not anymore.

When you have sex too soon in a relationship you were hoping had a promising future, then you run the risk of a few reactions, such as:

- Your partner will think, That was too easy. How many others got this far this quickly?

- Your partner will think, This person is great but not marriage material.

- Your partner will think, This is awesome. I really like this person and we are totally on the same page.

If you truly like this prospect, then I hope for your sake that his or her reaction is something like the third one in this list.

Contrarily, by waiting too long to have sex, you also run the risk of a few different reactions, such as:

- Your partner will think, I like this person, but I need to get laid, so I'm going to sleep with someone else in the meantime.

- Your partner will think, This person is a major tease and a prude, and we definitely are not a match after all this time.

- Your partner will think, Wow, I've finally met someone who respects me and sees sex as something more special than just getting off with someone.

Again, I hope your partner's reaction is something like the third example.

SEX SIGNALS: AFFECTION

Both men and women have been guilty of being super touchy-feely and then surprised when a date thinks they want sex. The line between touching someone's knee lightly to let them know you are attracted to them and moving that same hand up his or her leg toward his or her crotch is not a fine line; it is a very clear, very distinct, very obvious line. If you want to send an additional signal that you're interested without going anywhere near that tender area, then simply squeeze his or her thigh near the knee or make circles with your nails on his or her knee or move your hand to a safer place, such as his or her arm, and caress the forearm until you can gently place your hand in his or hers and intertwine your fingers.

Kissing needs to make a comeback. Remember those amazing make-out sessions you had when you were in high school and steamed up the windows in the car or hid in the den with the door closed so you would have a warning to disengage in case a parent walked in? Spend more time making out rather than rushing to have sex. You will build up even more anticipation, and, when you finally do the deed, it will be even more amazing. Make out sessions tend to be one of the first things sacrificed after real-life sets in. Once you are married with responsibilities and kids, people no longer find the time to just simply kiss without it being a means to an end (the end being sex). Kissing is foreplay, but let it be the type of foreplay that lasts for weeks before moving past first base.

Kissing is the best type of affection. You start off with that sweet nervous peck on your first date and move on to a two-minute make-out session on your second date and then a thirty-minute make-out session on your third date. Keeping your hands in the right places will ensure you don't take it further than you want to too soon. Touch the shoulders, arms, and neck. Run your fingers down his or her back. If you're sitting down, then touch the thigh right above the knee. Keep away from the chest and stomach. If you can't keep your hands off your date's body, then hold hands instead.

Sex doesn't always have to be "making love"; it can sometimes just be sex, whether it's with your significant other or with a date you don't see going anywhere. Sometimes singles just need to get laid, and that's okay, too. Many people have "special friends" they turn to in times of need, and as long as you don't hope that it will one day turn into something more, then there's no problem with having such a friend until you decide to get serious with someone. Don't wait until you're about to finally have sex with your new significant other to stop the "special friend" sex. Stop it as soon as, or before, you have The Talk with someone. For a "special friendship" to work, there needs to be complete transparency—be honest, be respectful, and be forthcoming. If you meet someone, just tell your special friend, and, if your relationship ends, then call your special friend and let them know you are available again and see if he or she still is as well.

What happens when you really like someone and can see a future with him or her but when you finally have sex it's awful? When there's been a lot of anticipation built up and the time finally comes to hit the home run, people tend to let their minds get the best of them. Give it another chance, even a few chances, before drawing any conclusions. If you really like your partner, then try to gently guide him or her in the position and rhythm you like, and be vocal with what is pleasurable and what is not. Some people simply don't know what feels good because no one has ever told them. Don't give up on a promising relationship right away until you have put in as much effort inside the bedroom as you did outside the bedroom to make what happens inside the bedroom be as good as things are outside the bedroom. Got it? This isn't always successful, but it can't hurt to try if everything else is going really well. The reverse situation—that is, trying to make a dull relationship better when the sex is great—more than often is not successful and is more than likely a waste of your time. Don't try to create a future where there isn't one. Enjoy the good sex for what it is.

It is difficult to disconnect one's emotions from sex. There's a reason Patti Stanger makes her clients in *The Millionaire Matchmaker* agree to wait until they're in an "exclusive, committed, monogamous relationship" before they have sex, and she recommends all singles should follow the same rule. Whether she's right or wrong, it's undeniable: Many people do tend to get emotionally attached quicker once they have sex with someone. This is why "special friendships" need to have honesty at their core, and it is also why I strongly recommend waiting before copulating.

....

 ### Julie

Julie isn't the type of gal who sleeps around and she would never have sex with a dud date even if she was attracted to him because she knows it isn't going to lead to anything. The last time Julie got herself some was the last time she was in a relationship, which was in her early twenties, more than five years ago! I don't think Julie is wrong for keeping her chastity, but I do think at this point she needs to loosen up. It is completely acceptable not to have sex with anyone until you're in a serious relationship, but she should also feel she can experience and enjoy some intimacy. Since Julie already enters dates expecting them to fail and then presents an uptight personality on top of that, she is not doing herself any favors.

As Julie's good friend and as a dating expert, I wish I could dress her for every event and every date, have a bug in her ear to feed her lines, and even have puppet strings on her arms and head to make sure she is looking at her prospects and touching them when necessary. Although she knows she's not going to sleep with any prospect until they are in a serious relationship, she doesn't need to let the guys know that through her body language. Being cold and rigid to let her dates know they are not going to get laid will only result in Julie not finding any connection or any forward momentum—not because sex is off the table, but because Julie's elbows are on the table, holding up her arms, which are crossed across her chest, solidifying the wall she has up.

♥ Natalie

After being wooed by Ben, Natalie doesn't want to move too fast, as she is really enjoying the blossoming romance. In her past relationships, including her marriage, she slept with guys too soon and always eventually regretted it. She feels a sense of comfort with Ben she has never felt with anyone, not even her ex-husband. She doesn't feel any pressure from him to move any faster, she is enjoying getting to know him without the distraction of sex, and she is really enjoying their lengthy make-out sessions.

Natalie is truly beginning to think Ben could be everything she has been waiting for, and he has already made nearly every man who has ever crossed her path pale in comparison. Natalie wants to wait a while before going all the way so that when they do, they are not just having sex but making love, as she already is feeling very deeply for Ben.

♥ Mike

Mike broke up with Kelly because he felt something was missing, and, now that he is single again, he is just looking to have fun. He is going out and hooking up with women, most of whom he will never see again. Mike needs to be careful that his rebound path doesn't cross with the paths of women he would date once he's gotten this phase out of his system. Mike is not ready to even reactivate his hidden profile on JDate, nor is he ready to attend Jewish mixers or ask friends to set him up. If Mike just wants to hook up with random women, then he needs to stick to the club scene and not take home women whom may have potential a few weeks from now when he's ready to start dating again. This is where Mike's twenty-one-year-old nightclub girlfriends can come in handy.

 ## Lauren

For Lauren, sex was the last thing on her mind after her divorce. She wanted to parent, enjoy quiet nights alone at home, and grab drinks with her girlfriends. Even once she was finally ready to date, she didn't care about having sex yet. Of course, she cared that the sex would be good once she found someone she wanted to have it with, but it certainly wasn't at the forefront of her mind. With Seth, Lauren was able to finally pop her postdivorce cherry. Lauren hadn't had sex with anyone but her husband for well over a decade, and she needed to experience everything from kissing to sex (and absolutely everything in between as well!) with someone else. For a while, Lauren didn't know if she wanted to wait and give herself to someone special whom she thought she would marry or if she just needed to get it out of her system. The latter won out in the end, and, even while Lauren had her doubts about Seth, she felt like he could help her cross that bridge. Now that Lauren has her first postdivorce sexperience out of the way, she doesn't plan on becoming promiscuous whatsoever, but the sense of relief she feels since that pressure has been removed is a positive.

 ## Beth

Beth and Andrea's plans to move closer together came to fruition with Beth getting the teaching position and moving to Milwaukee. They are trying hard to see each other as often as possible now that they are only a half-hour drive away. Their relationship isn't exactly long distance anymore, but, with their respective jobs and the drive, they still are not able to see each other day in and day out. They are in a committed and monogamous relationship now, and, although they know they have some growing to do as a couple since they don't see each other every day, they are thoroughly enjoying this time.

Beth and Andrea had gone all the way before they discussed moving closer together, and it was good . . . really good. After Beth moved, their sex life went from really good to awesome, which may have also been a reflection of their new level of commitment. Beth and Andrea are acting like teenagers who can't keep their hands off each other. When two people decide to dedicate themselves to each other, the emotional side infiltrates the physical side, and that can make making love better than ever.

♥ David

David and Karen are spending every day together and are talking about moving in together. David had only been with one person for thirty-five years, but, once he felt ready, he got out there and sowed some oats. David has been actively dating for a few years now but never met anyone whom he felt the urge to commit to. That didn't stop the women from convincing him they would still be willing to have sex with him, but that plan always backfired when David eventually found out the women were hoping the sex would make him change his mind and want a relationship. David felt bad, but these women were setting themselves up, since he was always honest with them. Then Karen came along, and he finally felt like he had met his midlife match.

Both Karen and David have the experience of long-term marriages, mixed with the confidence that age affords them, plus a desire to want to enjoy the second half of their lives. They're enjoying sex together on a frequent basis, which marriages of thirty years typically don't, and they're experimenting in bed (and on the floor and on the counter) in ways that marriages of thirty years typically don't. David and Karen have promised each other not to let this fun and active sex life dissipate when they do move in together. Everything else has been going along smoothly and hasn't felt like much work. But since they know serious relationships do indeed require work, they are going to dedicate themselves to working on upholding that promise of keeping their sex life fun.

Chapter 12

✶ BREAKING UP WITH DATING ❥

LET'S SAY THAT YOU ARE still on the market, still looking for that special someone. Month after month, the same faces
gaze back at you from the computer screen as you peruse JDate and
every other dating website, searching, hoping that a new face will
appear. And you pray this find will be a perfect match, with both of
you Favorite-ing each other, sending flirts and messages, exchanging phone numbers, and finally meeting up and realizing you've
found your beshert. But month after month this is not to be, and
your JDate prospects seem to be thinning as quickly as your boss's
hairline. Frustration sets in.

Event after event, the same people gaze upon you; you walk
through the door of yet another Jewish singles mixer and peruse
the crowds, hoping you'll catch sight of a new face and lock eyes.
You hold your breath as you make your way around the room, praying you'll find someone to spend the entire night talking to and
that the rest of the room will disappear into oblivion as you and
your beshert get to know each other. But event after event this

is not to be, and the probability of meeting someone seems to be dwindling as quickly as your bank account. Frustration sets in.

After so many dates, the faces sitting across from you begin to all look alike, and memories of the many evenings blur into a pool of redundancy, the chemistry always lacking, the conversation always boring. Even so, you hope and pray before each date that this time it will be different, this time your interest will be piqued, this time there will be instant attraction, this time you won't want the night to end. But date after date this is not to be, and the possibility of finding your beshert seems to be disappearing faster than the alcohol at an open bar wedding reception. Frustration sets in.

Most single Jews experience one if not all of these scenarios at some point (or at many points) during their dating lifetime. And it's not uncommon to experience all of them at the same time. All it means is that you need a break from dating, and you need it now. When the pressure is off, you can begin to clear your mind and shake off the awful feeling that finding your beshert is a hopeless endeavor, because it's not. Sometimes you just get stuck in a funk and need to get as far away from anything even remotely attached to dating, and that's okay. Talk to any of your single friends, of any gender, at any age, in any city, and you'll be quickly comforted by the fact that you're not alone in your misery.

There are many plusses to avoiding anything to do with dating for a while. For starters, when you reappear on the scene, you'll be that new face, and you'll see fresh faces as well. And your mind-set once you return to the dating game won't be one of frustration or desperation or resignation. Instead, you'll have a renewed sense of hope that all is not lost and that there is someone out there for you.

TAKE A BREAK

Every single eventually gets so frustrated with dating that they need to take a break. Taking a break is healthy, and it's a smart way to reenergize as long as you disengage properly. If you've been on JDate for the past six months and you've been to every single mixer for the past year and you've accepted every setup your friends and relatives have offered and are getting frustrated, don't worry—it's normal. When you've been too active in the Jewish dating circle, people have the tendency to assume you'll be present, and you'll actually start to blend into the crowd. Thus, making a timely disappearing act is necessary.

Taking a break means allowing your JDate (and any other online dating website) account to expire or canceling it even if you have time left on your contract (JDate does not allow you to freeze or hold your account). Since it may be too tempting to look at your prospects if you only hide your profile and make yourself invisible, I strongly recommend shutting down your account for the duration of your break. Taking a break also means not attending any organized singles mixers and not responding to people's requests to set you up (just tell them you're taking a break but will be in touch when you're ready). Taking a break means you are spending time alone to reflect, spending quality time with family and friends, getting in shape, concentrating on your career, and focusing on anything else you've been neglecting due to dating and its accompanying frustrations.

If your Facebook profile states "single," or "looking for a date," change it. You have the option to "hide" your relationship status on Facebook, so do so. It's simply not necessary information for the public to see. Once it's hidden, you can change your status without it getting broadcasted on your newsfeed. Or just leave the answer blank since you are not required to post it.

By changing your status technologically, you'll start to change your mind-set. Stop thinking about finding a husband or wife and concentrate on yourself right now. When you think about marriage every second of the day, it will seep through your pores and can alienate people. Stop looking at every attractive person you walk by and thinking, *Could that be The One?* Meet new people because they're nice, not because they're single.

Stop counting backward from the age you hoped to have children, stressing yourself out. You know exactly what I'm talking about: If you want to have kids by the time you're thirty, plus you want to be married a year before you have kids, plus you want to be engaged for a year before you get married, plus you need to date for a while before you get engaged . . . well, that means you have to meet your mate, when? Last year? Don't put yourself through this. When it happens, it happens, and it will happen. But it won't happen any sooner if you're frustrated with dating and emoting desperation or boredom. That's why breaks are not only healthy but also necessary.

Concentrating on your career, your health, and your relationships with friends and family will not only fill your time but will also make you a happier, more successful, more complete person. And that's the person who will attract the kind of man or woman you're looking for. But don't do it for your prospective life partner; do it for you. No matter how cute you think that line is from Jerry Maguire, you don't want your mate to "complete you"; you want him or her to complement you. Of course, when you're least interested in meeting anyone, you will start attracting attention, but make sure you're ready first. Dating takes a lot of mental work, and you must be strong enough before you get back out there.

When you do decide to reappear on the scene, you will be the center of attention. People will want to know where you've been, how you are, what you've been up to. They'll take new notice of you and will look at you differently. And you may discover someone new or even someone you have seen a million times on JDate or at a mixer that you hadn't noticed before because of the day-to-day dating doldrums. By stepping out from the scene, you'll return refreshed and rejuvenated, ready to take on the search with a better mind-set.

STUCK IN A FUNK

We all have those friends we see who are stuck in a funk. They're the people who aren't just single, they're S-I-N-G-L-E. They let their JDate account expire not because they are consciously planning on taking a break from dating but because they are just too complacent to bother extending their membership. These are the people who are always too tired to go out even though they seem to sleep more than most adults you know. These people are never in the mood to be set up or to attend a mixer and yet want so badly to be in a relationship that they can't even wrap their brains around the conundrum anymore. But hopefully something as little as taking a purposeful and effective break from dating will be enough to snap them out of this funk. Otherwise, if you think your friend may be dealing with something more serious than just a funk and you start to see other signs of depression, you may want to recommend that they meet with a therapist.

As a friend of someone stuck in a funk, you want to be there to help distract them and always invite them to join you, but these people are often so far into their own heads that they will almost always see your efforts as pity invites. One of the ways I try to help my friends who are stuck in a funk is by throwing them a "Celebrate You" party (like an Independence Party but with a much better name) to counteract the engagement parties, bridal showers, bachelor parties, weddings, baby showers, and kids' birthday parties they have had to attend—and buy a gift for—all while they were praying for a spouse and family.

If you're single and have been there for all of your friends through all of their simchas, why wait until you find someone to marry to register for gifts? Celebrate you for no reason other than that you're awesome and deserve to be showered with love. Of course, don't actually do it for the gifts, but do it so that people can let you know that you are loved and appreciated and valued. This type of celebration will hopefully be one of the things that helps you turn your negative attitude around and gets you ready for your reintroduction to the dating world at the end of your break.

Being single is not always easy, and it's definitely not always fun. Once you find someone, you get to start celebrating love left and right, but, when you're single, you don't get to do any of that. I can tell you that "your time will come" and that "patience is a virtue," as well as any other number of clichés, but the journey to finding a mate can be longer than and feel just as endless as any rabbit hole in *Alice in Wonderland* ("Either the well was very deep, or she fell very slowly, for she had plenty of time as she went down to look about her and to wonder what was going to happen next"). Such is the life when you're single, but, eventually, you will make it to the end of the tunnel and have a tea party to celebrate your engagement. Until then, make sure your friends schedule plenty of girls' or guys' nights out and hold conversations that don't revolve around weddings, babies, and buying houses.

Julie

Julie had a birthday last month, and, when it arrived, she became pretty darn blue. She didn't want to celebrate or go out or even answer the phone. She is literally the last one of her girlfriends to be on her way to marriage, and, as happy as she had been for everyone else, it finally got to her. It's sad. She tried so hard to be excited for everyone as they met their beshert and got engaged, got married, got pregnant, and so on, but eventually it exhausted her. I've been really trying to make sure the conversation doesn't always center on weddings and babies, but Julie doesn't seem to have anything else going on to fill the conversational void.

She's allowed herself to get totally immersed in her career, working fourteen-plus hours a day in a thankless job so that she doesn't have the time or energy to go out after work. She spends her weekends recouping, sleeping, and catching up on her recorded TV shows. I try to get her out for a girls' night, and still she hems and haws until I guilt-trip her into submission. When I try to discuss dating with her, a sense of defeat washes over her face and her body. It's difficult for me to empathize because, when I was single, I put myself out there, I went to all the mixers and networking events, and I was on JDate. I kept myself busy, too, but in social ways and in addition to work, exercise, and family.

To invoke Gandhi here, Julie needs to be the change she wishes to see in her world. She needs to make some changes to swing luck her way. For starters, she could lose those extra ten pounds she's always complaining about, or she could quit her job and find a new career that she's passionate about, or, at the very least, she could create a new

JDate account for the New Year. Any of these things would shift her paradigm, alter her outlook, and attract people toward her.

I know it's easier said than done, and I know it's easy for me to give advice since I'm not in her shoes, but I do remember how tough it was. And I know it will only get tougher for Julie if she continues to let being single get the best of her and if she continues to refuse to go out and meet new people. In the meantime, I will continue to be her friend, her sounding board, and her support system, and I will send every quality single Jewish man that crosses my path in her direction. I hope for Julie that she comes out of this break energized, enthusiastic, and ready to dive back into the dating pool headfirst.

 ## Natalie

Natalie is taking a different kind of break—a break from Ben. She explained to him, with intense emotion, that the break has nothing to do with how she feels toward him; in fact, she thinks she is falling in love with him, which is exactly why she wants to take a step back. She is not looking to go out and party or date anyone else or even spend time having cocktails with her girlfriends. Natalie just wants to reflect. She was permanently scarred by her divorce because she thought she really knew who and what she wanted back then, and since she was proven so blatantly wrong, she has a hard time trusting her instincts.

Natalie explained all of this to Ben, and he was very understanding. She doesn't believe she will ever meet anyone

HOW TO WOO A JEW

who is as good for her as Ben is or anyone who will make her feel as good as Ben does. Despite this, she needs time to make sure she's ready to take the next step with Ben and would rather deal with her issues now than freak out once they're engaged or married. Natalie doesn't doubt her feelings for Ben nor does she question his feelings for her; she simply is doing the soul-searching she wishes she had done when she was twenty-one.

Mike

Since Mike is out having fun and rebounding with women he would never think of dating—let alone marrying—he considers this a break from dating even though he's not depressed about the breakup. Mike had hidden his JDate profile while he was dating Kelly, so he let it expire after breaking up with her, and, now that he's sowed some wild oats, he is getting ready to create a new profile on JDate.

Creating a new profile after a relationship or a break ends rather than just reactivating your old profile is a better way to reintroduce yourself to the single community. Mike hadn't updated his old account for at least six months, and now that he took a chance by committing to Kelly (even though it didn't work out), he sees things differently and learned a little bit more about what he wants in a woman and from a relationship. Additionally, photos should be updated every six months, so this is perfect timing. Finally, a new profile name never hurt anyone. Women who may have viewed his previous profile on JDate (when it wasn't hidden, which was seldom) may not give him a second glance even with new photos and a new In My Own Words if his profile name is the same. By starting over completely, he will receive fresh views, some from the same women who were online before, some from women who are back from their own breaks and breakups, and some from new JDaters.

Lauren

Lauren has not been dating long enough to need a break, but her lifestyle itself has kept her marginally active in the dating scene. Because Lauren is so busy and not fully immersed in dating, she is experiencing a reverse effect. Lauren knows she isn't putting much effort into dating and that she will meet someone eventually, so she isn't stressing about it. The thing is, her being one step removed like this is attracting more men than she can handle. Lauren is flippant about the whole process, which means she is inadvertently playing hard to get, and men are drawn to her like bees to honey. Now, if only she had more of an interest in returning some of the phone calls, emails, and JDate messages. . . .

Beth

Beth took many breaks in her nearly thirty years of dating, and, now that she found someone she really likes, she's hoping she never has to take another break. Beth and Andrea live thirty minutes apart, so Beth is still able to maintain some independence, which is important to her since she has been single for so long and has depended on only herself for a long time. She is confident about her decision to move for a job she loves rather than a woman, and she is able to see how nicely everything is falling into place for her. Beth and Andrea haven't yet gotten annoyed with each other because they're not together 24/7, but Beth's not afraid what will happen if they do hit some bumps along the way. Beth feels as though she learned from all of her past relationships and mistakes and is being rewarded because she has shifted her priorities.

David

To David, as a widow who was married thirty-five years, a break is something you and your spouse take when you're in a huge fight and don't want to say something you'll regret. David and his late wife used to call a timeout when things got too heated, and one of them would take a walk around the block or take a bath or go for a drive. Then they would reconvene about an hour later when they could discuss whatever stressful issue was the source of contention. They learned about this timeout technique the hard way when they sought marriage counseling during their seven-year itch. David told Karen about the timeouts, and, although they haven't had a huge fight yet, they are discussing how they will deal with it when it happens, because they both know it will.

AN OPEN LETTER TO ALL MOMS AND DADS OF SINGLE ADULT JEWS

Dear Mommy and Daddy,

It's all your fault we're still single. You want to be grandparents so badly that you've pressured us into marrying a Jew at any cost. If you're wondering why some of us are well into our thirties with no serious significant other in sight, it's because of you. While we were growing up, you guilt-tripped us by telling us the Jewish population would die out if we did not marry another Jew, be fruitful, and multiply. You solicited Bubbe, the Rabbi, and a Holocaust survivor to tell us marrying outside our faith would be akin to finishing Hitler's work. You offered to pay for trips to Israel, for the memberships to join the Jewish fraternity or sorority, and for us to go to Jewish mixers.

You pointed out every single Jew that crossed our path, every Jew in a magazine or on TV or in a movie, and every Jew that was single at synagogue in September. You cut out the Jewish wedding announcements from *The New York Times* and read aloud the names of the bridesmaids and groomsmen, wondering aloud if they were also Jewish and if they were possibly single. You created and paid for a JDate account on our behalf (some of you secretly) and then emailed us the membership numbers of the ones you thought we'd like. You joined Facebook and asked about every person tagged in our photos. And you're surprised we date outside the faith or are still single?

Then, when we did bring Yids home, you pummeled them with questions about who their family is, what community they grew up in, what temple they belong to, and how often they attend. When someone's last name wasn't Jewish-sounding enough you mapped the family tree and then exclaimed triumphantly when you discovered their great-great-grandfather came from the same shtetl as our ancestors. You started asking other nosy questions: How serious is it, what's the next step, when would we settle down, where did we want to get married? You even suggested that it would be okay to procreate out of wedlock!

When we dated outside the faith, you said it was just a "phase" and hoped we would grow out of it soon. Those of you who are parents of Jewish gals would exclaim you were comforted by the fact that at least your grandchildren would be born Jewish. Those of you who are parents of Jewish guys would cry and ask G-D why you were being punished. You would hint to our significant others about conversion, sometimes asking outright if they would give up their faith for another. Would they be interested in becoming one of the Chosen People?

What you didn't realize is that dating is a journey of self-discovery, and, although some of us may take a long and windy road, many of us will end up right back where you wanted us: under a chuppah. But . . . some of us won't. Anyway, even if our spouses are Jewish, you aren't guaranteed to like them, and it doesn't necessarily mean the marriage will be successful!

The best thing about having Jewish parents is that we know deep down inside all you care about is our happiness, and we know you will still love us and care about us and accept us no matter whom we marry. And we know once we give you grandchildren, you'll get over it. But until we get there, please lay off and rest assured you ingrained in us the Jewish values we will eventually (hopefully) realize we want in our spouse.

With sincerest love and respect,
Your Single Adult Children

Chapter 13

★ JEWISH MOTHERS ➤

AS TONGUE IN CHEEK AS the preceeding letter is, it's also true. Jewish mothers are known for their meddling ways, and, though they're usually endearing, they sometimes get out of control. It's one thing for your mom to insist on paying for your JDate membership; it's quite another thing when your mom creates her own JDate account to pick out eligible men on your behalf. My mom did this when I was twenty-six years old. She logged on in secret, picked out who she thought was appropriate for me, wrote down their screen names, and then handed over the list. Curiosity ultimately would always get the best of me, so I'd log in to see who my mom thought was a good catch, and one after another I'd type in the screen names, and with each result I'd always be supremely disappointed. My mom got it all wrong: She picked guys who have been on JDate for years, guys who prey on every girl at local mixers, and guys who just simply aren't my type for reasons my mom should know and understand.

This isn't an uncommon scenario. Jewish mothers are great at promoting their kids, but, when they're trying to set their kids up on dates, it doesn't work so well. So many mothers have told me how handsome their son is, how successful, how funny, and so on, but, when I meet the guy, he's anything but.

I've found that many Jewish men have been given a complex by their mothers. They've been raised to believe they're better than the rest, can do no wrong, and deserve nothing but the best. That doesn't make dating easy. No woman will ever make him feel as special as his mother, and no woman can love him as much as his mother does. And those Jewish mothers don't have an easy time giving up their spot atop their sons' list of priorities and accepting the new woman in their sons' lives. But once you do get that much-sought-after approval of a Jewish Mother, you'll know you are loved, you are special, and you are in good—albeit nosy—company.

Jewish sons are not alone in their mother issues. Many Jewish women I know have not cut the umbilical cord. Their mothers go with them everywhere, they go to their mothers for advice or confirmation on everything even when they already know the right thing to do, and they even need to introduce dates to their mothers almost immediately for approval. When a man is finally welcome into the family, his mother-in-law-to-be doesn't fade into the fray. Mom will be there every step of the way, including through all the wedding planning, in the labor and delivery room, giving advice with raising her grandchildren (notice that they're "her grandchildren" and not "your children"), and basically inserting herself into her daughter's marriage. Accepting a woman's mother needs to happen well before the wedding day, as does the understanding that once again, this is a Jewish mother who loves deeply and generously . . . and without boundaries.

Telling your mom she doesn't understand because dating is different nowadays will get you nowhere. But it's true. Our parents didn't have JDate, they didn't have Google, and, on average, they got married a lot earlier in life than our generation does. But our moms have a point, too. The differences between men and women haven't changed since Eve took a bite of the forbidden fruit, and the ins and outs of dating remain the same as well.

Because of what I do for a living, many of my single friends—both male and female—are constantly asking me for advice. A lot of the time they have already asked their parents for advice, or were offered it (they are Jewish parents after all). And when my friends relay to me the advice they received and sometimes even followed, I am flabbergasted! From advising singles to admit how they feel too soon to telling them to lay all their baggage on the table, parents don't seem to have a clue about dating in today's world. Ask enough people for their dating advice, and eventually you'll hear contradicting statements.

My favorite is when moms tell their kids to "stop looking and you'll find someone." *Ummm*, no. Actually, not actively looking is detrimental to your dating life. The amount you're out there looking is directly proportional to how much you date. If you're not on JDate and other dating websites or going to Jewish singles mixers or accepting blind dates—or all of the above—then you're not going to meet someone. People meeting on the subway or at the gym generally only happens in the movies. Sure, it happens in real life every once in a while, but why sit back and wait for love to come to you? Instead, go out there and find it; otherwise you'll be waiting a long time!

The other popular piece of advice people get that I can't stand to hear is that they should try to be a "challenge." If you play hard to get, then how will you be gotten? I'm not saying to lay it all out on the line, but anytime you try to not try too hard, you're probably going to fail. When you pretend not to be into someone, your date is going to think just that—that you're not into him or her. Pretending like you're always busy will make the other person think you don't have time and are not willing to make time for him or her.

If you're offered advice from mom and dad without asking for it, or if you ask for advice but totally disagree with their answer, don't get into it with them. It's not worth it. Merely thank them for the advice and say that you'll take it into consideration (take note on this tactic because you will need it when you're planning your wedding and having children). Married people think that because they're no longer single, they know all. But just because a technique worked for them doesn't mean it will work for everyone else. Even dating experts get it wrong sometimes. See, I can admit when I'm wrong (hypothetically at least!).

Jewish mothers do have your best interests at heart, and the way to let them know they are both loved and appreciated is to set boundaries. The adult child of the Jewish mother who is overstepping her bounds needs to sit down and have a heart-to-heart with her. Let your mom know how much you love her, how much you can't wait to experience the next phase of your life with her nearby (just no longer directly at your side), and that you can't wait to turn to her for advice when needed. Explain to your mom that you plan on celebrating holidays together and having family dinners on a regular basis and allowing her to spoil her future grandchildren, but that there will be some laws laid down so your mom can be respectful of your marriage and parenting choices.

Julie

Julie finally moved out of her parent's house but still does everything with her mom, from shopping to manicures to dinner to spending the night back at home when she doesn't feel well or is down. Yet, when it comes to discussing dating, Julie's mom is persona non grata. Every time Julie speaks to her mom, her mom asks if she's dating anyone. Since Julie spends so much time with her mom, she is used to sidestepping the question or ignoring it altogether, but sometimes she makes the mistake of divulging information and then instantly regrets it. Suddenly she's bombarded with questions, the first of which has remained the same since Julie began dating at the age of sixteen: "Is he Jewish?" And if a relationship gets even slightly serious, Julie's mom will go so far as to Google the guy! And after the relationship ends, her mom will continue to ask about the guy, forcing Julie to recount how she was dissed by the guy or how he was such a dud date that she had to cut him loose.

If Julie tells her mom she has a date, she'll call the next day to ask how it went. Then she asks her for information Julie doesn't even reveal to her closest girlfriends. And when Julie refuses to tell her mom every last detail, her mom gets upset and says she never tells her anything. Julie's mom has no idea that Julie is annoyed by her pestering because, although Julie throws a slight temper tantrum in the moment, after things calm down, she never talks about how much it annoys her. Julie should chat with her mom during their manicures or after a yoga class when both of them are relaxed and let her know that she will tell her about boys when there's something to tell and that she will only divulge what she feels comfortable with and that she hopes her mom can respect her wishes to lay off.

Natalie

Natalie and Ben have reunited after Natalie's self-imposed break, and they have stepped up their relationship. Natalie, who lives at home, is taking Ben to her house to meet her family, and she's nervous because of what this step means. Since Ben will be joining Natalie and her extended family at her parents' house for Passover Seder, they have begun talking about their respective traditions and how they could combine them to create their own Jewish household. Natalie has a distinct feeling that talks like these plus a successful trip home will be the precursor to Ben popping the question.

Natalie is also nervous because her family is not exactly subtle. If Natalie's family has something to say, they say it—which is one of the reasons why she has always waited until she knows the relationship is serious and strong before introducing them to a new boyfriend. By this time, her mom has already Googled Ben and has researched what exactly it is he does, but her concern, especially since Natalie's divorce, is if a guy can take care of her. So what does Natalie's mom do? She's asks Ben if "he can afford her daughter." Great first impression, right? Natalie was mortified.

Natalie's dad is the quiet, brooding type who appears to have tuned out but is taking everything in. Although Natalie knows her dad only speaks when he has something to say, strangers find him to be intimidating. Natalie's dad also has an accent and is very smart, and these traits have always

 HOW TO WOO A JEW

rendered the few boyfriends Natalie has brought home speechless. Ben was no different. He was able to chat up Natalie's mom and charm her, but, when it came to talking with Natalie's dad, he clammed up. Luckily, Natalie warned Ben about her dad, and he knows that once he earns her dad's approval that the intimidation factor will disappear and the conversation will flow.

Natalie's sister is like some of the people described in "Embarrassing Moments" in Chapter 10: She will burp and fart no matter who is around. If a guy, whether he's her own boyfriend or Natalie's, can't handle it, then he doesn't need to marry in to their family. Natalie's brother is one of those guys who soaks up random information and regurgitates it to impress people with his smarts. And when the whole family is together and everyone is behaving true to form, Natalie usually loses her marbles and bickers with everyone, asking them to stop humiliating her. What Natalie tries to remember is that the few boyfriends she's brought home quickly became endeared to her family.

Natalie thought Ben handled her family really well and was able to relax in time for the second night of Seder. In the past, Natalie would have been nervous about taking a guy home and being scared that he'd feel pressured to have the marriage talk afterward, but, this time, she feels at peace. When Natalie saw Ben making her grandmother her special drink (vodka martini straight up, ice back, with olives on the ice) or discussing her grandfather's many hobbies (collecting precious gemstones, playing cards, and gambling on horses) or playing on the floor with her niece, it gave her a sense of warmth.

Mike

Mike has brought home just two women, the two long-term girlfriends he's had in life, with which neither relationship lasted more than a year. Mike waited to introduce them to his mom (who raised him on her own since his dad died when he was young) until what coincidentally ended up being the end of each relationship. Mike sometimes wonders if taking a girlfriend home is what puts the nail in the coffin of the relationship—meeting his mom means they expect the next level of The Talk and he just hasn't been ready for that. Maybe he was scared, but, if it had been the right girl, he wouldn't have been. Mike's mom is not a typical Jewish mother, but she did hem and haw over the two girlfriends because she desperately wants to welcome a daughter-in-law into the family. Mike also doesn't want to expose his mom to his philandering ways, and she has finally stopped probing him for information and is trying to be patient. Mike's mom is anxiously anticipating becoming a grandma and hopes he meets the right woman soon enough.

Lauren

Lauren is more willing to introduce prospective beaus to her parents than to her kids. Aside from joint playdates with a prospect's kids, Lauren will wait to introduce a man as someone serious only if she is considering marriage. As embarrassing as parents can make you feel, kids acting up are even worse. When one of her kids starts rebelling and she has to raise her voice in front of her boyfriend who has just met her kids, she is petrified at what he might think of her.

 HOW TO WOO A JEW

When another kid throws a ridiculous temper tantrum and she can't do anything about it, she is humiliated because she feels like it's a reflection on her as a parent.

It's these concerns that have led her to only wanting to date other divorced parents. Not only will they understand typical child behavior, but, when it is time to meet each other's parents, there will be a sense of comfort and familiarity. Lauren is also concerned about meeting the parents of a boyfriend who isn't divorced and doesn't have kids himself because she knows they probably hoped for something different for their son. Lauren's own parents were nothing short of excruciating when she brought home her ex-husband fifteen years ago: Lauren's mom would flirt with her boyfriend as if she were the single one, while her dad would open the door to their home wearing full hunting gear with a couple of rifles on the table behind him. Yes, some Jews are card-carrying NRA members. Luckily her parents have mellowed out now that they have grandchildren.

 ## Beth

Beth's mom, who died last year, was the stereotypical Jewish mother and was completely beloved by her five children, her daughters- and sons-in-law, and all her grandchildren. Her husband would roll his eyes at her shenanigans, but he adored her, and she endeared herself to everyone even as she licked her finger to wipe *shmutz* off their cheeks, straightened and tightened their ties, critiqued the short skirts, and asked potential suitors a million questions. Beth had brought home multiple serious partners (first boyfriends, then girlfriends), including a fiancé with whom she broke off a wedding. Now that she's met Andrea, she is devastated that her mom isn't here to love her as her own.

Beth's mom supported her completely and held her hand as she called off her engagement and then again as she discovered her sexuality and came out of the closet. Beth's mom tried to get her to lower her standards a bit and knew that Beth was making it impossible for a date to measure up, but she also knew Beth's strong will came directly from her. Beth could bring a date within five feet of her mom and know what her opinion was: She would crinkle up her nose at the faintest smell of cigarettes, raise her eyebrows at a disheveled appearance not fit to meet the parents, and purse her lips because of some other instinctual, intrinsic reaction (and she was always right). Every date Beth brought home, and every prospect her siblings brought home, knew exactly where they stood with Beth's mom. Even if she didn't make one of her trademark negative faces and actually liked the person, she still smothered them with questions. Surely she was annoying at the beginning, but, once there was a wedding, Beth's mom would treat her children's spouses as one of her own. Beth knows her mom would love Andrea and how happy she makes her and how well she treats her, and she has thought all along about how her mom would positively react to Andrea all through their courtship, which is what made her feel very comfortable moving to another state to be near her.

David

David doesn't need to worry about what his mother would think because he's old enough to not care. His mother was devastated when his late wife passed away five years ago and again when his father died last year at eighty-eight years old. But the sadness has not dampened her sharp tongue, which David has learned to laugh about after so many years. Karen has met his mom, and, after being warned by David that she is a witty woman, Karen was able to have fun with it all. Between the two of them, David and Karen have been through enough to not take things like that too seriously.

David's three daughters, on the other hand, are the ones whom Karen needs to seek approval from. They were plenty friendly even as they gave her the once over and listened intently to her every word, observed her every mannerism, and criticized her appearance. Luckily for Karen, she passed their tests, not only because she is eloquent, warm, and classy, but also because they saw how happy their Dad was with her. That didn't stop them from asking some difficult questions, but now, five years after their mom died, they are ready for their dad to find someone who makes him happy.

Chapter 14

★ JEWANNA GET MARRIED? ➤

YOU'RE READING THIS BOOK and have a paid account on JDate and are attending mixers and are poly-dating because you want to get married, or at least find a partner to spend the rest of your life with. Before you exchange rings under the chuppah, there are a couple more phases your relationship will have to go through, from meeting the ex, to moving in together, to getting engaged—all tests to see if your relationship is strong enough to withstand life's ups and downs.

EX MEETS NEXT

Most singles have some kind of past, whether it's other long-term relationships or a marriage, and, at some point, your past and present will collide. If it was a long-term relationship, chances are you still have some mutual friends and you might run into each other at parties. If you were married, then your lives will always be intertwined to some degree, especially if you have children together. When you move on to postbreakup or postdivorce, there will likely come a time when you will introduce your current love to your past love. It's awkward and can elicit questions and suspicions as well as incite competition.

Aside from having children with someone, there really isn't any reason to stay friends with an ex. Why do you want to see or hang out with someone you used to have sex with and shared intimate details of your life with? You may be okay with socializing with your ex when you're single, but, once you meet someone you see a future with, you will naturally lose the desire to be around your ex. Plus, you should respect your new partner enough to avoid putting him or her in a position where he or she would feel awkward. There are people who truly are friends with exes—their relationship ended eons ago and there is absolutely nothing between them—and if their current significant others are comfortable with the friendship, then that's great, but most people wouldn't be.

MOVE IT OR LOSE IT

Often people have a visceral reaction when they hear about someone upending their life to move across the country for love. Maybe it's cynical, but, when one half of a relationship moves for the sake of love, people tend to think the person is crazy for leaving his or her job, family, and friends all for the hope of a future. Sometimes these relationships work, and sometimes they don't. It's when they don't work that people like to say, "I told you so," but try to be sensitive about your loved one who had to swallow his or her pride and move back home after taking a huge risk.

There are a few signs to look for to see if you're moving for the right reasons or not. Did your significant other ask you to move,

HOW TO WOO A JEW

or did you offer? Are you moving all that way to move in together, or did your significant other ask you to get your own place nearby? Have you had The Talk yet? You should have no doubt in your heart or in your mind that you are moving because there is absolutely a future. Of course, that doesn't guarantee anything, but if you offered to follow your significant other to another city and he or she asked you to get your own apartment and you haven't had The Talk yet, then someone near and dear to you needs to smack you upside the head.

When your partner asks you to move for him or her and tells you he or she has already cleared the closet for you and says he or she wants to take this step forward in your relationship, then you're taking a risk that appears to have positive rewards. Whether you're moving out of carelessness or selflessness, you are taking a step that can mark the beginning of the rest of your life. If you're lucky enough to meet someone you believe is worthy, then why not sacrifice it all and follow the one who stole your heart to the ends of the earth to be with him or her? If you don't give all of yourself, then you have no one to blame but yourself. And if you move and get burned, then at least you know you tried everything to make it work and have no regrets. As Tennyson said, "'Tis better to have loved and lost than never to have loved at all."

MOVIN' ON UP

Halacha, Jewish law, does not support living together before marriage, as it shows a lack of commitment, but I believe moving into together is a major step in making the ultimate commitment in an educated manner. Imagine taking your vows under the chuppah only to move in together the next week and find you can't stand each other! What are you going to do, plead *kidushai ta'ut* (errors in the creation of a marriage based on information not being revealed)? People are able to put their best feet forward when you have separate residences, but, when you live together, you can't hide anything. You see the worst the other person has to offer—their moods, their habits, their messes—and you get to make an informed decision if that's someone you want to spend the rest of your life with.

Moving in together, even before the actual move, can be a good test for your relationship. Is one of you moving into the other's current place, or are you finding a new place together? If you're moving into your partner's place then tread lightly, as you might want to change things that he or she feels very possessive about. If you're finding a new place together, then you are suddenly combining finances and giving full disclosure about what you can afford and what your credit score is. In addition, you will also have to combine tastes and determine if you can merge your styles. You don't have to go to the extreme and make your place hyperfeminine or hypermasculine, rather find a way to compromise, which is a good lesson for the relationship.

What do you need, what can be donated, and what should be tossed out? If you are the one with the good taste and have convinced your mate to let you take charge, then don't let that go to your head. If your romantic roommate has the worst taste but has some family keepsakes, showcase those to give him or her an equal sense of ownership. If you take over the bedroom closet and all the counter space in the bathroom, then try to show some sympathy by relegating prime drawer space to your partner, since he or she will have to be traveling to the hallway closet to get dressed each morning.

Finally, I'm a big fan of trashing old linens and buying new. Fresh sheets + fresh towels = fresh start. Starting over is a good thing. You won't be able to convince anyone that no one else slept

("slept") in those sheets and your relationship deserves new 500-plus thread-count sheets and Turkish towels. (Or a visit to Target for a more economical version.)

MOVING DAY

Moving day is another normal occurrence that will allow you to bond as a couple because it's a time that is nothing if not stressful. From packing boxes to deciding what to keep and what to trash, deciding whether to rent a truck and ask friends for help or to hire a moving company (I've found that hiring the movers is always worth the money), and deciding where to put furniture and art to deciding which drawer should be used for silverware, it's all part of the process. After going back four times to buy more boxes because you underestimated how much stuff the two of you had combined, you are finally ready for moving day, and of course you've made the decision you'll later regret and rented the truck and begged a few friends to spend their weekend sweating away to move your crap, so now you're freaking out about every bump and scratch that would have been insured had you hired a moving company.

If you can escape moving day without fighting, then you can be very proud. And if you do fight but are able to keep it to a minimum by reminding yourselves that you're both stressed over the same thing, then you can also be very proud. If you're clawing at each other's faces and snapping at each other disrespectfully, then you may very well want to rethink not only the move but also the relationship. Between doling out who will do what to prepare for the move, to the move itself, to settling in after the move, the experience will bring you closer together. Having both your names on a lease and hanging a mezuzah together on the doorpost of your home and on your bedroom door will be monumental and symbolic.

ENGAGINGLY ENGAGED

Almost every relationship reaches a point where it's time to throw down the anchor or sail away—either you get engaged or you break up. Breaking up at this point can be heartbreaking and devastating because you've most likely been together close to a year and have hoped this would be the one. Don't let pride get in the way of staying together just because you have moved in together or are engaged. If you don't break up a bad relationship now, you may end up having to break off an engagement, which is going to be much more difficult. Many couples break off engagements because their passionate opinions on a specific topic—that should have been discussed long ago—differ. Are you committed to living next to your family regardless of where your spouse's career may take him or her? That could be a problem. Have you discussed the expectations regarding finances and how they will be handled when you want to buy a home and have children? Sometimes there are topics that are quite petty that end the relationship, though they are often just excuses for some bigger underlying issues the couple was afraid to address.

Priorities and preferences—even the ones that sound ridiculous to the next person—all need to be discussed before you make a commitment you can't follow up on. You may like how close your significant other is to his or her family but didn't quite realize just how attached he or she is, and how much their relationship would interfere with your relationship. You may like the idea of being married to a doctor but didn't quite realize that those types of careers require mobility and many hours, especially in the beginning.

You may think you want to go back to work after having kids and then change your mind once you actually have children, but your spouse (and coparent) doesn't agree. You can have cold feet anytime during a relationship, not just before a wedding. If you don't have these discussions before getting engaged, then have them before getting married. Better to swallow your pride and have to return a diamond ring then to get a divorce.

If you have survived technological miscommunications, polydating, and meeting each other's families, and if you have a great sex life and live together harmoniously, then you may want to put a ring on it. Getting engaged should be the happiest time in your life thus far (it will be usurped by your wedding and becoming parents, but for now this should be the highlight), and, if the thought of proposing to or accepting a proposal from your significant other scares you because you cannot see yourself living the rest of your life with this person, then don't propose or accept the proposal. If it's just the typical cold-feet feeling about taking that next step but you know you don't want to live without your partner, then don't live without him or her, and either propose or say yes.

The proposal isn't going to come out of nowhere, which means there will be opportunity to discuss the ring. You don't want to give a ring your fiancée hates, and you don't want to hate the ring your fiancé spent time and money picking out to surprise you with. So try to talk about it a little by popping into a jewelry store the next time you're at a mall and get an idea of each other's likes and dislikes. The proposal itself doesn't have to be extravagant, since the point is starting your lives together, but, if you do have an idea to make the proposal something of an event, then go for it.

Now that you're engaged to be married, there are quite a few tasks to add to your checklist. One of the most exciting things to do

CASHING IN ON YOUR RELATIONSHIP

A survey of experts from YourTango.com, an online relationship resource, found that the number one predictor of divorce can be attributed to differing values regarding kids, money, and sex. I've listed some difficult questions to ask about parenting earlier, and I discussed sex as well. Money is often a hot topic in relationships, but discussing how you view finances early on can prevent many arguments later. Answer these types of questions:

- Do you want to keep separate accounts or create one joint account?
- How will financial obligations be divided?
- Are either of you big spenders or sloppy spenders?
- Who is better at keeping track of paying bills on time and balancing checkbooks?
- How many children can you realistically afford? Can you afford to have one of you become a stay-at-home parent?
- If you're older and have a retirement fund, savings, and children, how does a new spouse fit into the financial picture?

Don't be afraid to ask the tough questions and discuss hypothetical situations. If you and your partner view money differently, you are more than likely destined for a difficult road ahead.

once you get engaged is to announce it to the world, calling all of your family and closest friends, changing your Facebook status, and flaunting your left ring finger whenever possible. Next, you ought to choose a date and send out save-the-dates to those whom you know you want to invite to your special day. You and your fiancé need to discuss what kind of wedding you want to have and who is going to take the lead on what.

Registering can be a lot of fun, and you should do the first round of registering together. It's important for both of you to be included in this process since these will be items you are going to fill your matrimonial home with. When you're discussing the wedding, make sure you always say "our" wedding, not "my" wedding. It sounds like an obvious tip, but you'd be surprised how easy it is to slip up. Planning a wedding can be very stressful, so try to always remember what the point is: The two of you starting your lives together and celebrating your love in a ceremony and party ripe with tradition.

Weddings are times when people's commitment to Judaism is strengthened. Planning a ceremony under the chuppah with seven rotations, performing a *bedeken* ceremony with your veil, signing the *ketubah*, smashing a kiddush cup, wearing a *talit* or a *kittel*, hearing the seven blessings, and placing the solid band on each other's right pointer finger are all actions your parents took, their parents took, and their parents took. Then of course you have the party where you get to revel in dancing the hora, getting lifted up on chairs with a napkin connecting you and your spouse. All these things are a beautiful way to begin your life together.

♥ Julie

Julie has been on a bunch of dates with this guy named Zack that she met on JDate. On their fifth date, he came to her place to pick her up and asked her if it would be okay if they stopped by a friend's house for an hour before dinner because a bunch of his friends were getting together. She said sure, and they headed off. It wasn't until he rang the doorbell that he told her the hostess was his ex-girlfriend. *Um*, thanks for the heads up! Zack explained they've been "just" friends for a couple of years and she has a serious boyfriend now. Still, Julie was stunned. It wasn't a huge deal, but it would have been better if Zack were straight up about whose party it was from the start. There was no going back at this point, so Julie pasted a smile on her face and introduced herself to the hostess.

Zack's ex-girlfriend was incredibly friendly with Julie, and she tried to get chummy with her. But in an effort to befriend Julie, the ex made some inappropriate comments and asked some inappropriate questions. She tried to bond with Julie by asking her if she ever felt annoyed by waking up in Zack's bed to find his dog lying next to her. Well, this only being Julie and Zack's fifth date, she hadn't yet spent the night at his place but didn't feel that was information she needed to share. Then the ex told Julie she wished that Zack would teach her new boyfriend how to give a body massage. Again, this was not an experience Julie and Zack had shared yet, and Julie found the entire situation incredibly awkward. Finally, the ex boasted to Julie that it's because of her that Zack uses ChapStick and has soft lips. Thanks for the 4-1-1, lady.

 HOW TO WOO A JEW

Julie relayed this story to me, and I've given it some thought. I think the ex may still have feelings for Zack and that he either is oblivious to this or is just playing dumb. They have so many mutual friends now that to admit he knows she has feelings for him will make things awkward in their group. Regardless of whether or not the ex has feelings for him, how soon is too soon to introduce a new date to an ex you now happen to be friends with? If you have to lie about where you're going until you're at the door, then it's too soon. If you're still able to count the number of dates you've been on with your new prospect on one hand, then it's too soon. If you haven't yet had The Talk, then it's too soon. If your ex doesn't know how to be nice without being totally inappropriate, then it's too soon. If you have any inclination your ex might still harbor feelings for you, then it's too soon. This goes for both girls and guys. Meeting an ex is intimidating, and it's even more so when the ex mentions intimate tidbits.

Julie was a class act and didn't exchange any information besides to say that she and Zack had just recently started dating. She also didn't mention any of this to Zack because she didn't want to start any trouble. It bugged her, and she is filing away the information in the back of her mind just in case there any other red flags in the future, but the experience didn't eliminate him from being a dating prospect. After all, it was his ex that was acting classless, not Zack. I told her that in the future if Zack were to ask if she wanted to hang out with his friends that she should nonchalantly ask which ones before agreeing. If the friends once again included his ex, she should say that she'd rather just hang out with him one-on-one instead. No guy is going to have a problem with that!

 Natalie

Natalie and Ben have been discussing marriage, and Ben came right out and asked her if there was any diamond cut she wouldn't like. She told him "princess" because it was the cut she received from her ex-husband. He understood and appreciated that she wanted something new and original with him. They also discussed what kind of wedding they would have since she had already had one but he hadn't. They decided they would invite no more than one hundred people, that they would pay for it themselves, and that, if their parents wanted to contribute, they would use that money to begin their joint savings account. This was going to be their wedding, celebrating their love and their future, and they weren't going to cater to anyone's requests.

Then one day, Natalie received another card from Ben in the mail, which started her on a scavenger hunt. The first card included a hint for a location in their city, and, when she got there, she found another card with another hint. She moved from location to location, finding a card at each place that contained yet another hint. Each location she visited was somewhere they had gone on a date at the beginning of their courtship, and, finally, ten cards later, the scavenger hunt ended back at her home, where Ben had lit dozens of candles and strewn rose petals in a path from the front door out to the back yard, where he waited for her on bended knee.

Natalie and Ben are planning a wedding for next summer, long enough for them to save more money and to attend plenty of sessions with their Rabbi, something Natalie failed to do with her first marriage and insisted on this time around.

Mike

Mike turned thirty-four last week and attended a wedding of one of his closest friends, and he realized he has few single friends left. This was quite the wake-up call to Mike, as not only does he have no one to go out with, but he's also seeing less and less of his friends because they'd rather be with their wives or with other couples. In the past this would have bugged Mike and elicited a couple-hating rant, but this time something was different. This time, he looked around from his lonely spot at the singles table toward the tables filled with his friends and others their age with their girlfriends, fiancées, and wives, and he was jealous that they had someone to sit next to, share dessert with, dance with, hold hands with, whisper inside jokes to, and look at (and be looked at) with total acceptance and adoration. Suddenly Mike wanted that, and he wanted it bad.

Mike returned home and went right to work on his JDate profile, paid for six months, and activated the account so that it was viewable to the public. He found the community calendar online and registered to attend a few of the upcoming mixers and hobby groups, and he sent an email to a few friends to let them know he was finally ready and very serious about meeting someone . . . someone Jewish, at least twenty-five years old, nice, fun, smart, sweet, and, let's be honest, attractive. Mike knows he isn't going to meet her overnight, but he does have hope that now, with the right mind-set, it will happen sooner rather than later.

Lauren

Although Lauren had a big, over-the-top wedding complete with an engagement party, three bridal showers, and a bachelorette party, that was nearly fifteen years ago. If Lauren met the right guy, she would most definitely get married again. The wedding would be much different—smaller for starters, and without the big wedding dress, but it would also be more intimate. The wedding Lauren had was planned for and paid for by her mom, with help from her former mother-in-law, and Lauren was only too happy to let them take the lead. This time, she would want it to be much more personal and would of course include her kids, as well as any future stepchildren, in the planning process and the ceremony. Since Lauren has decided she only wants to date other divorced dads, she understands that any wedding will be a union of two families and wants their modern-day Brady Bunch to be together under the chuppah. Lauren has already thought out a lot of this but isn't putting any pressure on herself to make it happen anytime in the near future. When it happens, it happens. Lauren loves being a single mom, working, exploring her new identity . . . and even dating.

Beth

If I had heard about Beth moving for Andrea a few years ago, I would have rolled my eyes and asked her if she was crazy, moving to another state for a woman without a ring! But Beth made this decision on her own terms, she has grown exponentially throughout her dating decades as well as by dealing with the loss of her mother, and she finally had her priorities straight when she met Andrea. The fact that Beth loves Andrea more than she loves her hometown of Chicago is a clear example of how much she has changed, and for the best.

Singles can learn a lot from Beth. It took thirty years and lots of dud dates and heartbreak, but Beth came out on top. Andrea decided Beth was worth the commute since she had moved states for her, and so she left her small town and they moved in together in Milwaukee. The couple has learned more about each other since moving day than ever before, and they have survived. They divvied up the responsibilities that go into taking care of a home. Andrea actually volunteered to wash the floors, take out the trash, and clean the toilets (Beth's least favorite things), while Beth does the laundry, the dishes, the dusting, and the vacuuming. They trade off cooking or do it together.

They discovered who gets testy when she gets hungry, who gets pissy when she gets tired, and who leaves her dirty clothes everywhere. They've also discovered that none of those things bother them enough to make a big deal out of it, and now that they know they can stand each other twenty-four hours a day, seven days a week, Andrea has proposed! Beth's Dad handed her an envelope when she and Andrea came home to Chicago to celebrate their engagement, and inside was a letter from her mom written before she died full of advice for her on her wedding day, as well as a check to pay for the wedding. Beth had come to terms with the fact that she may never get married so this letter and check held incredible sentimental value that her mother always believed it would happen for her.

Although neither Wisconsin nor Illinois recognizes their union, they are planning a ceremony on the shores of Lake Michigan. The temple they belong to is Reform—although they were both raised Conservative and there is a Conservative Rabbi who performs same-sex marriages, they both feel a sense of belonging with the Reform congregation. The ceremony will be traditionally Jewish and symbolic by nature and neither Beth nor Andrea need more than that until Wisconsin or Illinois will issue them a marriage license. The couple plans to split the gender-specific roles of a typical Jewish wedding equally to signify their equality in their relationship.

 ### David

David doesn't care about getting married again, but he would do it if Karen wants to, which she does. So David and Karen have decided they will do a small backyard shindig with their kids and a few close friends and relatives. Karen will wear a cream-colored sundress and walk down the aisle barefoot, and David will meet her under the chuppah wearing a matching cream-colored button down with jeans, also barefoot. Their kids will give them away, and, after a short ceremony, they will feast on BBQ and dance under the stars.

Neither David nor Karen thought they would ever find love again, though the reasons they each became single were very different. Meeting each other and taking vows

    HOW TO WOO A JEW

solidifies that what they have together is fulfilling and real even though they both had very fulfilling and real relationships that lasted for many years prior. What made them both realize this was a union that could work is that they never compared each other to their first spouses the way they did with every other date they each went on. They accept the fact that they both deserve to find and fall in love again, and it doesn't take anything away from the significance of their previous marriages.

✳ YOUR DESTINATION ➤ IS YOUR DESTINY

WHEN YOU'RE A KID OR a teenager, you have a romanticized notion of love. You think you're going to marry your high school sweetheart and that whatever it is you're feeling is "true love." Heartbreak is the end of the world, and you can't imagine living when it happens to you. Eventually you do get over it and realize there are many more fish in the sea.

When you're in your late teens and early twenties, it is time to have fun, and at twenty-one you can start meeting people at bars and clubs. Alcohol is introduced as part of dating, and, in your early twenties, dating is more akin to partying, as alcohol allows you let your guard down, sometimes too much. From the age of twenty-five through your late twenties, you start to take dating more seriously as you look for a mate and not just a date. The daunting age of thirty is quickly approaching. You always thought you'd be married by thirty! You sign up for online dating, accept blind dates, go to the Jewish singles mixers, and basically do everything you said you would never do—and thought you would never have to do—in your early twenties. You start to think about what you want in a spouse much more seriously. Your list is long, and no one can meet your standards.

Once you hit thirty, the race is on. You realize certain traits are not quite as important as others, and, although you're desperate, you also realize how much you've accomplished in other areas of your life and are proud. But you start to question what is wrong with you instead of what is wrong with your dates. Introspection leads to independence.

By forty, frustration becomes a huge part of dating. Where are all the singles, and why aren't you meeting them? Your preferences now include divorcés and a much wider age range than you ever imagined. You start to come to the conclusion you may never get married and you may never become a parent, and you convince yourself that is okay, even though deep down inside you are mourning the life you thought you would have. This mind-set allows you to date people who may not have the genetic pedigree you preferred earlier in life, since you're not looking at someone with reproduction in mind.

At fifty, you're now at a place in life where you enjoy what you have and are no longer dwelling on what isn't. You travel, you have close friends, you are successful, you are independent, and you are happy. You would love a companion to share your life with, but the standards by which you are judging someone are no longer as stringent or superficial as they were half a lifetime ago. You are looking for someone you get along with who also has some similar hobbies but is just as willing to try new things as you are. You aren't thinking about planning a huge wedding with a white dress but rather finding someone whose life can blend with yours to create something magical and comforting.

Everyone has his or her journey. Some people meet and marry their beshert at the same time they graduate college and end up having long and successful marriages. In this day and age, with women having illustrious careers and bearing children at a much older age, the twenty-one-year-old bride is not the norm. Although the idea of marrying your high school or college sweetheart sounds endearing, only in retrospect will you see how much growing you have to do before you can find your match. What you think is important when choosing your senior prom date sounds infantile ten years later when you're making The List. Back then, you cared where your date was going to college, and not because of how good the school was but how close or far it was from the university you were planning on attending. Back then, you cared about staying committed and loyal through freshman year and not acquiescing to temptation. You envisioned getting married as soon as you graduated college and having kids right away and being successful, but you had no idea how that would all actually happen because you hadn't yet had the life experience that would come to help you comprehend the big picture.

Couples I know who did get married in their early twenties went down two paths: They either grew up together as they were raising a family or they grew apart. There's a reason people say that life doesn't begin until you're thirty (some even say it doesn't start until fifty!) because until then, your view of the world isn't based on life experience. Love is this intangible thing equated to butterflies in the stomach and the thoughts of not being able to live without each other. Once you reach your thirties, you realize that love is something you build upon. Yes, you want those butterflies, and, sure, you don't want to live without each other, but you also know that butterfly feeling eventually goes away and that, if you do have to live without the other person, you will survive.

A visceral reaction called attraction brings you toward each other, but you can't build a lasting relationship on just that. Commonalities are imperative, and the most important one is religion. When you have Judaism as a foundation, you can build a marriage, a home, and a family upon it. That doesn't mean you won't get divorced, although, as we know, the divorce rate for Jewish innerfaith marriages is much lower than the national average.

There is a connection within Jew-on-Jew love that you will be hard-pressed to find with someone who was raised differently. A non-Jew may sympathize but not be able to empathize with why you can't drink beer on Passover even if no one else will know. He or she may not understand why you can't even take a nibble during Yom Kippur fast if no one else sees you (because you will know and you will lay the Jewish guilt on yourself for doing so). He or she won't know why gefilte fish is a must-eat delicacy a few times a year, or why it is a sin to put mayonnaise on a corned beef sandwich or put anything but sour cream or apple sauce on a latke. He or she won't know how to smile and nod patiently at the Jewish mother's inane opinions, or know the hand motion accompaniments to Birkat HaMazon, or understand your obsession with pointing out every Jewish celebrity who graces the cover of a magazine, stars in a TV show, or is featured in a movie. He or she won't understand the need to overcook and overbake for the holidays no matter how many people are coming, or the pride you get when another Jew wins a Nobel Prize or another popular invention comes out of Israel, or how in the world you can get drunk off Manischewitz.

Julie, Natalie, Mike, Lauren, Beth, and David all had differing journeys and some have found their beshert, just as I had my unique path and you will have yours. I hope that you can connect with the advice laid out here—or advice from anyone—and be able to learn from it in order to prevent you from making too many mistakes. That said, some mistakes aren't mistakes at all. For instance, my first marriage wasn't a mistake because my son is a product of that marriage, I learned some incredible life lessons, and I've now met my second (and, G-D willing, last) fiancé. It was just a few months after my divorce that we met, but, because of the lessons I had learned about what kind of husband I needed and what kind of wife I could be and what kind of coparent I was looking for, I was able to identify him right away. I had also learned from my first marriage to trust my instinct when it came to discerning the stories I was told during the initial getting-to-know-you phase, and I was able to ask the right questions. My fiancé and I both had learned about not sweating the small stuff, compromising, and being flexible. Since we are both single parents, we introduced our kids during a playdate, and not only were we both able to see how the other parented, but we could also see how our own child reacted to the other adult as well as the other child in the room. Over time, we were able to start seeing how our lives could mesh together and began talking about what we each wanted in the future. We are now planning our life together as a reality, not just a fantasy, and it includes marriage and more kids.

Beshert, I'd like to reiterate, doesn't mean soul mate; it means destiny. It could be that your beshert is to be a frustrated single, like Julie and Mike, who needs to reassess what your priorities are in your own time so you can be a better version of yourself, which will allow the right person to eventually come along. Your beshert could be a second marriage, like Natalie, whose first marriage ended in divorce and heartbreak and created a deep distrust of men until someone showed her how she is supposed to be treated and how she deserves to treated. Your beshert could be an acceptance of being alone, like Lauren, who left an unhealthy marriage and found a strength within herself she never knew existed. Your beshert could be to be alone or at least accept the possibility of being alone—not having kids and never getting married—like Beth, who only found her soul mate after surviving the unending "When are you going to get married, dear?" questions from yentas and realizing that the important thing in life is being happy in your own skin. Your beshert could have left you a widow at a relatively young age, like David, who never thought he would be able to see the light of life again until he realized no one would ever replace his late wife and that he needed to enjoy the rest of his life in her honor.

Your destiny may be to never get married, or it could be that you did everything possible to meet a Jew and yet fell in love with your non-Jewish colleague, or it could be that you become a single parent. Jews believe that your destiny is already written in the Book of Life, but it is up to you to make life what you want of it. If you say, "It will happen when it's meant to," I'm afraid it will only get you so far. If you're sitting at home alone, at least keep yourself company with a JDate account. It's time to go after your destiny.

✶ ACKNOWLEDGMENTS ➤

THIS BOOK WOULD NOT HAVE been possible without the help of so many people. First, thank you to my agent, Hannah Brown Gordon at Foundry Literary + Media, and my editor, Laura Mazer, along with the entire team at Seal Press/Perseus for your support and guidance. Thanks to Debra Kamin who gave me the opportunity to write my first dating column—I don't think either of us knew where we were going to end up just five years later! A huge thank you to my family for pushing me to reach farther and take my writing to the next level. To all the guys who weren't my beshert: Thank you for sending me weird emails, taking me on awful dates, and even rejecting me via text message—this book wouldn't exist without you. And finally, to my four guys, I love you all more than you will ever know!

⭐ ABOUT THE AUTHOR ➤

© tracy renee photography

TAMAR CASPI has been writing for more than ten years in nearly every medium. She has written for FOX Sports Net, E! Entertainment Television, the Outdoor Life Network, Clear Channel Communications, and the San Diego television news affiliates of ABC and NBC.

Since 2008, Caspi has written an internationally syndicated Jewish dating advice column that appears in publications such as *The Jerusalem Post* and regional Jewish magazines and newspapers around the United States. She has been JDate's official blogger for the past three years, where she doles out dating advice, gives profile makeovers, and offers a lifeline to the lovelorn.

SELECTED TITLES FROM SEAL PRESS

31 Dates in 31 Days, by Tamara Duricka Johnson. $17.00, 978-1-58005-366-2. After another in a long line of painful breakups, Tamara Duricka Johnson vows to go on 31 dates in 31 days—and to resist the urge to turn each date into her next potential relationship.

Otherhood: Modern American Women Looking for Love, Marriage, and Motherhood and Finding Instead a New Kind of Happiness, by Melanie Notkin. $16.00, 978-1-58005-521-5. Melanie Notkin shares the funny, sexy, and sometimes heartbreaking stories of today's well-educated, successful women who find themselves childless in spite of their desire to be mothers.

Screw Everyone: Sleeping My Way to Monogamy, by Ophira Eisenberg. $16.00, 978-1-58005-439-3. Comedian Ophira Eisenberg's wisecracking account of how she spent most of her life saying "yes" to everything—and everyone—and how that attitude ultimately helped her overcome her phobia of commitment.

1,000 Mitzvahs: How Small Acts of Kindness Can Heal, Inspire, and Change Your Life, by Linda Cohen. $16.00, 978-1-58005-365-5. When her father passes away, Linda Cohen decides to perform one thousand mitzvahs, or acts of kindness, to honor his memory—and discovers the transformational power of doing good for others.

Yogalosophy: 28 Days to the Ultimate Mind-Body Makeover, by Mandy Ingber. $18.00, 978-1-58005-445-4. Celebrity yoga instructor Mandy Ingber offers a realistic, flexible, daily plan that will help readers transform their minds, their bodies, and their lives.

We Hope You Like This Song: An Overly Honest Story about Friendship, Death, and Mix Tapes, by Bree Housley. $16.00, 978-1-58005-431-7. Bree Housley's sweet, quirky, and hilarious tribute to her lifelong friend, and her chronicle of how she honored her after her premature death.

Find Seal Press Online
www.SealPress.com
www.Facebook.com/SealPress
Twitter: @SealPress